NATIONAL SECURITY
An Overview

NATIONAL SECURITY
An Overview

Edited by
Sankar Sen

NATIONAL SECURITY: An Overview
Edited by Sankar Sen

First Published 2016

ISBN 978-93-5002-425-6

Published by
AAKAR BOOKS
28 E Pocket IV, Mayur Vihar Phase I, Delhi 110 091
Phone: 011 2279 5505, 2279 5641
info@aakarbooks.com

Laser Typeset at
Arpit Printographers, Delhi 110 092

Printed at
Saurabh Printer, Greater Noida

Contents

Introduction

National security has been defined as the capability of a nation to use its national power for the protection and preservation of its unity and integrity and furtherance of core values and national aims and objectives. Internal security, which involves threats of various dimensions faced by a country within its borders come under the rubric of national security. Today, national security of India is imperilled by different disruptive and destabilizing forces intending to tear the country asunder and block its progress and development.

Admittedly, India is in a violent neighbourhood facing threats of various dimensions to its national security from its neighbours. With a view to breaking India by thousand cuts, Pakistan is aiding and abetting cross-border terrorism by jihadi outfits. It has made terrorism an instrument of its foreign policy and seeks to achieve through terrorism goals that it cannot realize in fields of battle. The Mumbai carnage of 26/11 was the high-water mark of Pakistan-sponsored terrorist attacks on India during the last two decades.

Prime Minister Narendra Modi's peace initiatives so far have not paid dividends because of the opposition of the Pakistan army to mend fences with India and give up its support to India-specific terrorist groups operating from Pakistan. Hence, threats to national security from Pak-sponsored terrorism continue and Kashmir remains a flash point. Periodic interdiction and neutralization of terror modules in India, underscore the continuing threats posed by cross-border and home grown varieties of terror. Another development of great concern is that the toxic doctrine of violent jihad is attracting educated radicalized youth seeking excitement and adventure. Emergence of ISIS has made the jihadi world bipolar with a battle for ascendency between Al-quaeda and ISIS. The ISIS and al-quaeda rivalry has reached Pak-Afghan border and may cause consolidation of jihadi ideology in this region.

India's relations with its other neighbour Bangladesh have improved; but the situation inside Bangladesh remains volatile with the two Begums locking horns and the fundamentalist groups whipping up communal and sectarian frenzy, seeking to strengthen nexus with their counterparts in India.

The illegal infiltration from Bangladesh poses another serious threat to national security. It is a matter of great concern that different political parties in India have encouraged it to strengthen their vote banks. Unabated illegal infiltration has changed the demographic complexion of the border States like Assam and West Bengal. Ram Ohri's article in the book makes an in-depth analysis of this looming threat.

India's relations with the other giant neighbour China, remains uneasy and fraught with problems. China now wants to cultivate better relations with India, which offers a vast market for its manufactured goods. However, China is not prepared to resolve early its border disputes with India. Arunachal is shown in map as part of China. While China has settled border disputes with Myanmar with a few minor rectifications, in case of India, it covets large chunks of Indian territory—the largest territorial claims against any nation so far. China is also making huge investment of nearly 40 billion dollars for building road and rail links from Xinxiang to the port of Gwadar in Pakistan. Despite terrorist violence convulsing Pakistan, China is going ahead with the project because it wants to use Pakistan to keep India off-balance. Hence, the present display of Chinese bonhomie should not create any illusion of lasting friendship. China's ambition is to become the sole great power in the region and it will not allow India to emerge as a competitor.

Another weak pillar in our national security architecture is the poor health of the Indian police. The Indian police for a variety of reasons and causes has become dysfunctional and unable to adequately grapple with the serious threats and challenges to national security. There is acute shortage of police personnel in India. There are approximately 122 policemen per 1 lakh of population, which is far below the police-population ratio in peaceful and advanced countries of the west. In states seriously rocked by naxalite violence, like Orissa, West Bengal, Jharkhand it is even less than 100. It is disturbing to note that the police-population ratio improves in urban areas. Vast expanses of rural countryside remain neglected and go without any policing worth the name.

Articles in the book, penned by experienced and well-known police officers, highlight the urgent need for police reforms with a view to insulating the police from extraneous political pressures, forging close co-ordination with the private security agencies and streamlining the functioning of the state armed police battalions, many of which have become effete and ineffective. Indeed, good policing is *sine qua non* for ensuring national security and good governance, and any qualitative improvement of policing in the country is not possible without police reform and reform of the criminal justice system.

Thought-provoking and wide ranging articles in the book carefully examine a wide gamut of issues concerning national security with incisive comments and suggestions. It is hoped that the book will be of great interest to the law enforcement officers, security experts as well as informed members of the public.

Sankar Sen

1

Bangladesh: Liberation Interrupted

Bhaskar Roy

Bangladesh is an independent country no doubt, but has it attained liberation?

It is unfortunate that this question is still asked even 43 years after independence. In its fight for independence from West Pakistan, Bangladesh (still East Pakistan in 1970) lost approximately three million lives including old men, women, and children. The huge impact of this tragedy appears to be largely erased by those who, either openly or covertly opposed independence.

The War of Independence in 1971 is also known as the war of 'liberation'. The expression 'liberation' is at the heart of the issue. East and West Pakistan were incongruous twins born with religion as the yardstick used by the British. The two wings of Pakistan had nothing in common—not in language, culture, way of life or even the practice of religion. Religion in the two wings differed greatly. While West Pakistan tried to identify itself with the Arab countries, and in its practice of religion, adopted a more rigid version of Sunni Islam, religion practiced in the eastern wing was a more accommodative Sufi tinted Sunni Islam.

West Pakistan tried to overwhelm the East through

various means. Language and cultural imposition by the west was strongly resented among the Bengalis of the East. The language movement in 1952 against the imposition of Urdu was the first expression of discontentment that snowballed into the liberation movement. **The Bengalis sought 'liberation' from the language, culture, religion, and the way of life from the dominant Punjabis of the west.** This 'liberation' was at the heart of the independence movement seeking 'democracy' and 'secularism' as platforms to practise the rest. These ideas/precepts were enacted in the first Constitution of Bangladesh. And these ideas are currently under severe challenge.

There are two parts to the atrocities committed on the people of Bangladesh in 1971, though both are interconnected. The Pakistan army was the major force on the ground against the independence movement. The other was the Bangladeshis, both Bengali-speaking and Urdu-speaking (known as Biharis), who were known to indulge in violence against women and other weaker sections like old men, children, and religious minorities, such as the Hindus.

The Jamaat-e-Islami (JEI) and its students' wing, the Islamic Chaatra Shibir (ICS), earlier known as Islami Chaatra Shangha, were responsible for creating killing organizations like the Razaakars, Al Badr, and Al-Shams. Collectively known as 'collaborators', they continue to press their agenda forcefully even today, with able assistance from some, who can be called Pakistan's Trojan Horses.

The first Constitution of Bangladesh (1972) enshrined secularism as a state principle, banned political parties based on religion, and declared Pakistan's collaborators in 1971, ineligible for election to parliament. Consequently, JEI ceased to be a political party. Top JEI leaders like Gholam

Azam and Salauddin Qader Choudhury fled abroad. Their Bangladeshi citizenship was revoked. Most other JEI leaders were put in jail.

Rise of the Trojans

In the early hours of 15 August 1975, a group of young army officers killed Sheikh Mujibur Rahman and his entire family living in Bangladesh. Only his two daughters, Sk. Hasina and Sk. Rehana who were abroad, survived.

The assassination of Bangabandhu was a conspiracy extending beyond the borders of the new nation. Two key players, who emerged were Khandakar Mustaque Ahmed and Taheruddin Thakur. Both had concealed themselves in the top level of the Awami League, and Sk. Mujib's council of ministers. Khandakar Mustaque became prime minister on 20 August, and Ziaur Rehman took over as Chief of Army Staff on 25 August, after eliminating the incumbent, Gen. Khaled Mosharraf.

Thereafter, it was Gen. Zia who controlled events of coups, counter coups and the amendment of the Constitution. Gen. Zia became president of the country on 21 April, 1977. All sections in the Constitution proscribing the JEI were revoked, their leaders released from jail, and the party jumped into politics. Zia also formed his own party, the Bangladesh National Party (BNP) in 1978.

Pakistan's influence in Bangladesh was substantially restored; the clock on 'liberation' determinedly turned back, and pro-liberation elements cornered. Today, we see Bangladesh divided between pro-Pakistan/Islamic fanatics and pro-liberation/secular forces.

Terrorism

Islamic fundamentalism took roots in Pakistan from the very

early stages. In Bangladesh, it was sponsored by the JEI and ably supported by Zia and President H.M. Ershad. It reached its pinnacle during the BNP-JEI rule of 2001–06. The Afghan Taliban actions and the '9/11' Al Qaeda attack in the US, greatly enthused and encouraged them.

The BNP-JEI top leaders dismissed questions on the terrorist organization Jamatul Mujahidin Bangladesh (JMB) and its leaders as a creation of the media. The countrywide bomb blasts (in 63 out of 64 districts) on 17 August, 2005, changed the narrative. A warning from US President George W. Bush forced Prime Minister Begum Khaleda to arrest the top JMB leaders, who were executed during the caretaker government rule. Several BNP-JEI ministers involved with terrorists were under arrest and being tried. The JMB and its leader, Siddiqul Islam @ Banglabhai, received patronage from ministers like Aminul Haque, Alamgir Kabir, Lutfozzaman Babar, Ruhul Quddus Dulu, and others.

In operational terrorism, senior intelligence officers were also involved. Northeast Indian separatist militants like ULFA and NSCM (I/M) were not only given sanctuary in Bangladesh but also facilitated to procure arms, ammunition, and explosives.

On 30 January, 2014, a Chittagong court sentenced 14 to death in a case of smuggling 10 truckloads of arms and ammunition which landed at the Chittagong Urea Fertilizer jetty on 01 April, 2004. The arms were destined for the United Liberation Front of Assam (ULFA) in Assam. Those sentenced, included Motiur Reheman Nizami, JEI Amir, and former Industries Minister, Lutfozzaman Babar, former Minister of State for Home, former National Security Intelligence (NSI) Chief Rezzakul Haider Choudhary and others. Rezzakul Haider was also a close aide of Tareque Reheman, Begum Khaleda Zia's older son and a BNP leader.

This case, however, goes wider and deeper. Pakistan's ISI was also directly involved in it. It was supported by a Pakistani telecom company, ARY, which had done money laundering for the Al Qaeda, according to reports. Tareque oversaw the operation. The arms came from China. The ambit of investigation in this case is likely to be expanded and may net other opposition heavyweights.

Equally disturbing were the attacks on Sk. Hasina's life. In this also, BNP-JEI direct involvement has been reported. According to a study in 2004, Bangladesh had at least 125 terrorist organizations. They received foreign funding and JEI was the facilitator. Most effective were the Harkat-ul-Jihad al-Islami (HUJI), Jaish-e-Mohammed, and others with Pakistani connections.

Although Sk. Hasina has greatly reduced active actions of most of these organizations, they cannot be easily uprooted. The danger is still there, and they are waiting for their mentor to return to power.

The rise of political Islam in Pakistan, which was patronized by the army, created a mirror image in Bangladesh. It was frequently argued that Islamic parties like Jamaat hardly ever won seats of consequence in the election and were, therefore, hardly any threat. This is not true. The mixture of political Islam (fundamentalism in politics) and the powers that be (like the army) created an explosion in Pakistan, the reverberations of which can be felt even today. The genie was let out of the bottle. The government, Islam, and the army in Rawalpindi have lost control to jehadis and Talibans in large tracts of the country.

Bangladesh should have learnt from the Pakistan experience. But parties like the BNP, the Jamaat, and their associates have learnt a negative lesson. The year 2004 stands out as the year of terrorism in cooperation with the

BNP-Jamaat government. The countrywide bombing by the JMB, the assassination attempt on the Awami League president Sk. Hasina, the smuggling of 10 truckloads of arms into Chittagong on 01 April, destined for Indian insurgents, and several political assassinations, were remarkable.

But little seems to have changed in the BNP-Jamaat camp. This was clearly demonstrated in the run up to the 05 January, 2014 parliamentary elections.

Minorities

Hindus are the largest minority in Bangladesh followed by Buddhists, who are mainly located in the Chittagong Hill Tracts (CHT). Hindus are spread all over the country. Christians are a very small group left in the backwaters. The relationship between the Muslims and the minorities is complicated, and has roots in history. There is a pre-partition background, a post-partition period from 1947 to 1971, and then post-Independence period from 1971.

The plight of the Hindus deteriorated as a consequence of an increasingly political Islam. Yet, it is also necessary to state the fact that there was a very close relationship between Hindus and Muslims, with mutual respect towards each other. In the cultural area, there were Hindu *baul* singers and Muslim *mafrati* singers, both of whom had the same message—*Why lock up your gods in mandirs, masjids and churches*? There are many such examples.

The other issue is of land. The population to land ratio is very small. Hindus possessed a lot of land, but they were the weaker group. Added to this is the hard-line religion pursued by the radical Jamaat and the like.

The Hindu population was 22 per cent in 1951. In 1961, it was 18.5 per cent. It reduced further to 13.5 per cent in 1974, 12.13 per cent in 1981, 11.62 per cent in 1991 and 9.6

per cent in 2001. Major Hindu exodus took place in 1947–48 during partition, when many Muslims, too, moved from India to East Pakistan (Bangladesh). During the War of Independence in 1971, 10 million refugees moved to India, and 80 per cent of them were Hindus. Many did not go back. Since then, periodical upheavals, including the recent riots have forced Hindus to sell their immovable properties and seek a new life in India.

But this is not the whole story. Hindus have lived and are still living with dignity in Bangladesh. Hindus have not only joined the Awami League but have also supported it. Hindus are also found in the BNP and left-oriented parties. There are professors, judges, civil servants, and army officers, who are Hindus, and they do not want to become refugees. It is this writer's experience that, in the regular flow of life in Bangladesh, language, culture, and nationalism transcend religion.

It would be a pity if the Jamaat extremists are allowed to root out Hindus. The multi-religious and multi-cultural palimpsest of Bangladesh is its greatness.

Political and Social Stability

Unfortunately, political and social stability eluded Bangladesh from almost the very beginning. Sk. Hasina, who was already into politics when her father and family were executed in 1975, returned to Dhaka only in 1981. She was unanimously elected as President of the Awami League. With Bangabandhu Sk. Mujibur Rahman and most other top level independence movement leaders assassinated in 1975, she became the symbol of independence, and the mantle fell on her shoulders. In the perception of anti-liberation forces both inside and abroad (read Pakistan mainly), Sk. Hasina's leadership is the glue that keeps the pro-liberation forces together. Hence, she must be removed or eliminated, according to her opponents.

The parties opposed to independence were powerful, and still remain engaged in the affairs of Bangladesh. Pakistan, of course, is the primary mover, though some Pakistani intellectuals are veering to the fact that the Bengali revolt was their own creation. But the Pakistani army, the Inter Service Intelligence (ISI), and Islamic radicals are not reconciled with the *status quo* as evolved. Within this also is the fire in the heart to dismember some part of India, that is, Kashmir or Northeast India or both! The (1971) US National Security Advisor/Secretary of State, Dr Henry Kissinger, took the break-up of Pakistan as a personal affront. He was supported to the hilt by President Richard Nixon. It is not only that the US aircraft carrier 'Enterprise' was dispatched to the Bay of Bengal to support the Pakistani troops, but it is alleged that the US even considered the use of the nuclear bomb against India. It was a ridiculous idea, yet one that was nevertheless considered.

Kissinger got his revenge with the assassination of Sk. Mujibur Rahman. The US prosecuted its relations with Pakistan for a number of reasons and continues to do so. This is a geopolitical reality.

After '9/11' and the declared war on terrorism, it was expected the US would counter organizations and political parties like the Jamaat and its associates. Unfortunately, it is playing a bizarre game. It continues to call the Jamaat-e-Islami a moderate Islamic political party. No comments have come from the US on the trial in the 21 August, 2004 case regarding the attempt to assassinate Sk. Hasina, in which 22 senior Awami Leaguers were killed, or on the creation of Hiffazat-e-Bangladesh, which along with the Jamaat demands Sharia law in Bangladesh or even on the Jamaat's own stand on religion and the Constitution.

If the US is trying to prove to the Islamic world that by supporting Jamaat-e-Islami it is not anti-Islam, it will not work. Its support will drastically impact political and social security, stability, and religious harmony in Bangladesh. The immediate impact will be suffered by India, but the disastrous consequences will also flow out of South Asia to other countries.

The foreign interference in the 1971 war crimes trial is, to say the least, disappointing. The horrors of killing and rape by the Pakistani army and their East Pakistan (Bangladesh) collaborators (the Jamaats), in 1971 must be brought to a conclusion.

Although the US and the European Union (EU) have not challenged the truth of the happenings of 1971, they tried to derail or at least postpone the proceedings by trying to find inadequacies in the International Crimes Tribunals (ICT-I and ICT-II). The bitter irony of Bangladesh's post-Independence history is the fact that those very people and organizations, who were against 'liberation' and were defeated, would come to rule over the victors. This could not have come to transpire without a powerful conspiracy between internal and external forces.

Unless the ghosts of 1971 are put to rest and the remaining culprits punished, Bangladesh will have no stability. The anti-liberation forces are continuing to sprout new generations that are equally determined to do what their predecessors did. Any encouragement to them from any quarter would be like pouring fuel on fire.

The 'Minus Two' Formula

The 'minus two' formula came into vogue in Bangladesh in 2007–08. At the time, several articles were written, the objective of which was to oust both Sk. Hasina and Khaleda

Zia from politics, since the two leaders carried baggage and could not get alongwith each other at all. During the military-backed caretaker government, both leaders were briefly jailed on charges of corruption but subsequently released and the charges withdrawn. There was a move to push both leaders out of the country, but it did not succeed.

Periodically, there have been talks of a step-by-step approach of 'minus one' at a time, the first candidate being Sk. Hasina.

Alternate leaders are not clear. But a Wikileaks disclosure of a US dispatch said that Dr Md. Yunus, Nobel Laureate and the father of microcredit finance, which empowered poor women, was a possible American candidate. The matter had apparently been discussed with him by US officials.

During her brief stopover in Dhaka as US Secretary of State, Hillary Clinton made it clear that Dr Yunus was a friend of the US and her personal friend, and she strongly objected to Sk. Hasina's government ejecting Dr Yunus from the Grameen Bank created by him.

It is true that Dr Yunus briefly flirted with the idea of forming a political party. It is also true that Sk. Hasina made Dr Yunus' life difficult.

Whatever may be the situation at present, there is an uncanny feeling that the 'minus' formula thinking in whatever form has not been fully withdrawn. Is there a 'regime change' policy for Bangladesh? The result could be as disastrous as being seen in Iraq.

The India Factor

Geography cannot be wished away. Nor can history. India surrounds Bangladesh with a common land border. Or, as BNP foreign minister Morshed Khan said in 2004,

Bangladesh also surrounds India. Khan's statement was an open threat to India through the use of insurgents and terrorists.

Historically, a line was drawn by the British to separate a large piece of land on the basis of religion, which then became Bangladesh. With the same language and similar culture on both sides of the border, it is impossible that events in Bangladesh would neither affect, nor involve India. The BNP-Jamaat government actively supported Pakistan in terrorism and insurgency in India.

India-Bangladesh relations under the Awami League-led government showed sparks of promise, but met road bumps at every stage. Although the process may have been slow in many areas, thankfully nothing has been derailed.

Although it took Prime Minister Sk. Hasina a full year after elections to visit India, the time was well spent by the two countries to make the visit substantive and meaningful. The joint statement signed between Prime Minster Manmohan Singh and Prime Minister Sk. Hasina in New Delhi (12 January 2012) was an agreement on a vision for the future, in pursuit of the common good—bilaterally, regionally, and globally.

A large number of areas of cooperation were identified including starting the '*Maitraee* (friendship) Express' railway service from Kolkata to Dhaka as well as several other projects of mutual benefit.

During Dr Mannohan Singh's visit to Dhaka in September 2011, a slew of agreements and MOUs were signed between the two countries, which included India's assistance in Bangaldesh's hard-pressed power sector. Already, 250 MW of electricity is being transferred to Bangladesh from Bheramara, West Bengal. This is expected to rise to 500 MW. The Chief Minister of Tripura, which has become a power surplus state, has recently offered to sell 100MW of power to Bangladesh. India also granted an assistance of US$ one billion for various developmental projects of which US$ 200 million was later converted into an outright grant.

A proposal, very important for India, which has been stalled by the Bangladesh opposition, is the land corridor to India through Bangladesh to the Northeast region. It was argued that India could use this corridor to move its troops to the Northeast to strengthen its borders with China, and this would make China unhappy with Bangladesh! The question of Bangladesh's sovereignty was also raised. Even the purchase of power from India was objected to. A major promise concerning India's security that Prime Minister Hasina made and delivered on was clearing the country of anti-India terrorists and Indian insurgents. None exist today in Bangladesh, and those arrested have been handed over to the Indian authorities.

India's internal politics derailed two high priority agreements. One was the Teesta river water sharing agreement. West Bengal Chief Minister Mamata Bannerjee objected at the last moment, though she had no real reason to, not even vote bank politics. Nevertheless, she was miffed with the central government.

The other was the Land Border Agreement (LBA). The LBA was signed in 1974 in the Indira-Mujib accord. The Bangladeshi Parliament ratified it. To ratify the agreement, the Indian Parliament had to make a constitutional amendment, to which the BJP objected.

There is huge potential in India-Bangladesh relations, but this can be exploited if only negative politics is kept out of the way: for example, land transport connections between Nepal, Bhutan, and Bangladesh through India and surplus power from Nepal and Bhutan to Bangladesh through India. These can be achieved with reciprocal action from Bangladesh.

Geographically, Bangladesh is ideally placed to form a link in the chain of Asian connectivity from India to South East Asia. But the Asian Highway, supported by the Asian Development Bank (ADB) is locked with objections from Bangladesh. These issues are resolvable. What is required is political will, and a commitment on India's part. India also must discharge its responsibilities.

Conclusion

Today, Bangladesh is sharply divided politically and ideologically. BNP's closest partner, the Jamaat-e-Islami, has been banned from contesting elections by a High Court order as the organization refused to abide by the country's Constitution and Election Commission guidelines. The Jamaat demands Sharia law for the nation.

The BNP avoids this question, sticks to the Jamaat, and some BNP leaders sometimes say the two have ideological commonality. The divide has grown to such an extent that the BNP-Jamaat are beginning to openly support Pakistan (thus indirectly denying the 1971 genocide in Bangladesh).

In Bangladesh's political discourse, the proximity of the Awami League to India is emphasized, and for good reasons. India had to intervene militarily in 1971 after the Pakistan Air Force bombed the Agra air force base. Even otherwise, all top liberation leaders took refuge in India openly, and for some time, the Bangladesh government-in-exile functioned from Kolkata. India hosted 10 million Bangladeshi refugees, standing by the cardinal values of democracy, secularism, and humanity.

India also reached out to the BNP in the interest of

bilateral relations and non-interference in Bangladesh's internal affairs. Unfortunately, the BNP, under Begum Khaleda Zia and her son Tareque Reheman, carried out anti-Indian activities, aiding terrorism and insurgency. Very recently, after the 05 January, 2005 elections, Khaleda Zia supported a report in a pro-opposition daily, that Indian soldiers were brought to Satkhira to quell riots! A charge that the ruling government of Prime Minister Sk. Hasina had sold the country's sovereignty to India.

Such a position adopted by the second largest party in the country towards its immediate neighbour can only portend many more problems to come.

It is time that Bangladesh's major donors review the situation inside Bangladesh. They must know that the Jamaat is not by any measure a moderate Islamic political party.

The following are issues that need very careful handling with foresight:

(i) Social indicators point to the fact that Bangladesh is no longer a Less Developed Country (LCD). It must be allowed and helped to attain its millennium development goals.

(ii) Influential external forces must desist from political experiments. This region does not need a mini Iraq.

(iii) Any thought from outside for regime change must be discarded forthwith. Let Bangladesh settle its own political issues.

(iv) It is the responsibility of all countries fighting terrorism to ensure Bangladesh does not descend to becoming another haven for terrorists, particularly, since it almost became one.

Bangladesh is a very important player in South Asia and the

SAARC. It is also a gateway to the East, not only for India, but also for South Asia. The next two to three years are going to be a stressful time for Bangladesh. A complete resolution of the pernicious developments of the past is required. There can be no halfway measures and patchwork solutions.

A stable Bangladesh is in the interest of all concerned.

2

The China Factor in India's Security

Kalyan K. Mitra

More than 50 years have passed since the border war with China shook the country. Thanks to the media, the bitter memories of the military debacle are still very much alive in our minds, while we keep forgetting that global and regional politics have changed fundamentally in the intervening years. It is time we take stock of current ground realities and figure out what lies ahead for the two Asian giants instead of going back to the humiliating events of the past at regular intervals. China and India are two rising powers of Asia with a combined population of two and a half billion or more. Although it is difficult to predict how powerful these two countries will actually be in another 10 years, it is reasonably correct to assume that both are destined to play a much greater role in Asia and the Indian Ocean region in the years to come. The economies of both these countries are estimated to grow despite global slowdown. China has done considerably better than India, having begun its economic reforms much earlier; it has already displaced Japan as the second largest economy in the world. China's military modernization has kept pace with its spectacular economic progress. Growing economic strength and military muscle have inevitably shaped the strategic thinking and world view of post-Mao China's leaders.

The 18th Congress of the Communist Party of China (CCP) installed the new 'Fifth Generation' of leaders with 59-year-old Xi Jingping as the General Secretary as well as Chairman of the Party's Central Military Commission (CMC). He also took over as President of the People's Republic of China in March 2013. The leadership change in China was more or less smooth despite reports of intra-party manoeuvring and intrigues before the Congress was finally convened in November 2012. The all-powerful Standing Committee of the 25 member politburo has seven members, six of whom have degrees in subjects like economics, law, and history. One member is a technocrat having specialized in military engineering. The new Central Military Commission (CMC) has 12 members, two of whom are from the Standing Committee of the Politburo and the remaining ten from the People's Liberation Army (PLA).

The new state leadership was formally installed at the 12th National People's Congress (NPC) on 16 March 2013. Xi Jingping and Li Keqiang took over as the State President and the Prime Minister respectively. As expected, the NPC made it clear that there would be no experiment with political pluralism while China would go ahead with the task of revamping the economy. The party's rigid control would be maintained and greater attention would be paid to rooting out corruption, ensuring good governance and social harmony. The NPC also reconfirmed that the party would continue to keep the PLA under control and command the gun, so to say. To describe Chinese polity in one or two words, I can do no better than quoting the renowned sinologist, Harry Harding, who described post-

Mao China as a 'consultative authoritarian' system which is no longer focussed upon the charisma of one paramount leader. It is authoritarian because the system will suppress dissent to keep intact the party's iron grip on political power.[1]

The 18th Central Committee of the CCP held its much talked about Third Plenum in November, 2013. It adopted an ambitious, comprehensive roadmap for reforms covering almost every sector—economic, social, legal, and military. These reforms will have to be implemented by 2020 in order to realize the 'Chinese Dream' of renewal and rejuvenation as proclaimed by Xi Jingping. The Plenum marked the emergence of Xi Jingping as a leader wielding considerable authority and signalled the beginning of a new style different from the collective leadership political system seen during the post-Deng era so far. The bold reform package in which Xi was directly involved contains sweeping economic reforms accompanied by elaborate security controls. There will be a 'Leading Group' to design, implement, and monitor the reform programme along with a 'National Security Committee' for coordinating the different instruments of state security to ensure that the reforms do not endanger social stability or the primacy of the Communist Party. These two powerful bodies at the central level, outside the normal party and state hierarchy, will strengthen the power and authority of Xi, to whom they are expected to report.[2] Several noteworthy Plenum decisions include, inter alia, abolition of the labour reform camps, ending the *hukou* or the urban registration system, relaxation of 'one child per family' rule, and removal of barriers to population mobility. The primary focus of the Plenum was on economic reforms, but crucial reforms relating to national security were also approved. On the economic front, a 'decisive' role has been accorded to market forces in the allocation of resources. If and when implemented, this could herald the shift from an investment-driven pattern of growth to a consumer demand-driven one and competitive pricing for oil, gas, water, power, transportation, and telecom services. Far-reaching major military reform measures approved by the Plenum relate to streamlining of personnel and reorganization of military leadership structures. Briefly stated, the reform proposals approved during the Third Plenum aim at lifting China to the level of the world's most advanced nations by the year 2020 and enable the country to realize the 'Chinese Dream'.

For the new leaders of China, internal stability and social harmony will top the agenda for action because social unrest and repeated clashes between peasants and officials have assumed alarming proportions on account of nepotism and corruption by party officials in a period of growing urbanization. These vital domestic issues will keep the new leadership busy in the foreseeable future. The crucial dilemma for china's leaders today relates to the future of ideology. The appeal of the communist ideology had already begun to lessen during the Deng era. His successors are facing growing signs of instability and slackening of the party's grip. The economic reforms have brought about major changes in people's attitudes towards the party and the government. The ever-widening economic disparities, rampant corruption, unfulfilled expectations of higher living standards, and a host of other factors have given rise to public cynicism, resulting in frequent unrest and protest. If China fails to reverse this trend and ensure that the fruits of economic reform are distributed evenly in a corruption free society, the legitimacy of the rigid one-party system and the relevance of the Communist Party will diminish further. The emergence of a civil society consisting of professionals and private entrepreneurs in major cities and coastal areas have led to a visibly weaker presence of the party and the state in many sections of society today. Powerful local stalwarts are often able to lobby effectively and defy central directives. As the ideological appeal of the party declines, China's leaders will be further discouraged from experimenting with political reforms. The experience of Gorbachev's Soviet Union and the former East European states have demonstrated to the ruling elite in China, the dangers of toying with political pluralism, which has great potential for destabilizing the polity: hence, the dominant concern with stability in any discourse on national security. And nowhere is it better illustrated than in China's White Papers on National Defence, which are published biannually. The scenario for the future, therefore, will be tight political control over dissident activities along with gradual, incremental pluralism in both social and economic spheres. China seems determined to prove that one-party dictatorship can coexist with market economy though empirical evidence teaches us that a Marxist-Leninist polity is fundamentally incompatible with a market system. Hence, only time will tell for how long China will be able to prevent the inevitable interaction of economic and political institutions.

Centrifugal forces and ethnic friction are not likely to present unmanageable threats to the internal security and stability of the Chinese state. No doubt, there is serious disaffection in the Tibet Autonomous Region, where the government has encountered periodic public protests, self-immolations, and riots by the local people. These have been ruthlessly suppressed, but the problem persists. In Xinjiang, there has been separatist violence and unrest over restrictions on the practice of Islam. Inner Mongolia has also witnessed unrest from time to time. But unlike the former Soviet Union, which could not resolve the historical incompatibility of the Slavs, Baltics, Transcaucasians, and the Central Asian peoples, in China, the Han Chinese are an overwhelming majority, accounting for nearly 93 per cent of the population. They have been systematically settled in various Autonomous Regions over the years. In Inner Mongolia and Xinjiang, they actually constitute a majority. Nevertheless, China cannot afford to ignore ethnic and religious separatist movements altogether. It views the growing Islamic fundamentalism in Pakistan and some of the bordering Central Asian Republics with concern. The ruling elite, of course, can count on the People's Liberation Army (PLA) to bring overwhelming military force to safeguard the unity and integrity of China in a crunch situation. The PLA has done so in the past—protected China's sovereignty and sustained the one-party rule whenever called upon to do so.

Although the PLA leaders have almost disappeared from the front ranks of the party with no representative in the all powerful standing committee and only two in the 25-member politburo, the PLA remains a very important, albeit somewhat invisible, force for China's leaders with more than 30 percent representation in the party central committee. The recently created 'Strategic Planning Department' within the PLA's General Staff Department is believed to be handling non-military diplomatic matters as well. The PLA is reemerging as a behind the scene player insofar as vital territorial and maritime issues are concerned. The present generation of PLA leaders are educated, technology-savvy professionals who are keen to ensure that China achieves rapid modernization of the armed forces and enhances its military power. Most of them seem convinced that the Western powers and USA in particular will weaken China by promoting dissent and separatism. Interestingly, despite divergence on the issues of pace and extent of economic liberalization, the political leadership and the top military brass are quite united on the issues of national defence and military posturing. The strategic thinking of China is based on the concept of maximization and management of Comprehensive National Power (CNP) and exploiting to maximum advantage the relative configuration of external powers. The approach enables China to measure its national standing vis-à-vis the relative power of other nations. Consequently, China seeks strategic leverage by exploiting rivalries and manipulating relations with other sovereign states in pursuance of its national objective to prevent the emergence of a dominant power or alignment of powers opposed to China.

China's strategic goals are as follows: developing the capability to deal with military contingencies relating to Taiwan, safeguarding maritime interests by dominating South China Sea and the East China Sea, furthering capability to deal with India across the Line of Actual Control (LAC) and protecting the vital oil supply route from West Asia & Africa in the Indian Ocean through rapid modernization of its Navy. USA is the primary target of China's defence planners followed by Taiwan, Japan, and India. India does not figure all that prominently in China's radar. In China's strategic calculation, North-East Asia and the South-East Asian region are more important than South Asia. Since its South Asia policy has India at its centre, China has systematically developed close ties with India's neighbours. All of India's neighbours have obtained much of their military arsenal from China. China sees South and South-East Asia as areas where India is its rival and likely competitor. The Chinese strategic thinkers have lately begun to worry about the visible upswing in Indo-US relations, which has the potential of altering the geo-strategic landscape in the Asia Pacific Region.

Is the logic of geopolitics pushing India towards a strategic alliance with the US to contain China? There is speculation in many quarters in India and abroad about India's place in America's global strategy vis-à-vis China. There are signs that the USA is working with India in a way it has never done before. A number of breakthroughs on defence sales have paved the way for a long term defence supply relationship. The Indo-US defence cooperation has political and strategic objectives in dealing with power equations in Asia and the Indian Ocean. There is an Indo-US agreement to secure maritime trade routes between the Suez and the straits of Malacca. However, there are several question marks on the strategic logic of US-India relations in the context of a rising China in the Asia-Pacific region where the US is seeking to project itself as a 'Pivot of Asia'. Can the US help India in transforming its potential capacity into actual strength so that India can play the role of a balancer vis-à-vis a rising China? Should India, along with Japan, Vietnam and Indonesia try and seek a regional equilibrium in order to induce good behaviour on the part of China? India has genuine fears about getting entangled in Washington's problems with Beijing. It may be a better idea for India to identify and seek possible convergence with China in the Indian ocean stretching up to the Pacific to ensure freedom of the vital sea lines of communication and energy security instead of confronting China to promote America's strategic goals in the region. More importantly, one should not take it for granted that the US is planning to pursue policy with a view to containing China.

Policymakers in the US and knowledgable commentators have repeatedly stated that America is not seeking to contain China. Washington recognizes that the rise of China as a world power is unstoppable and its cooperation is necessary for addressing regional and global concerns. Any attempt to contain China will be counter-productive because it will not only divide America's South-East Asian allies but may have the opposite effect by encouraging China to withdraw into narrow aggressive nationalism. As Joseph Nye Jr. has very aptly remarked, if America treats China as as enemy, it will guarantee a future enemy.[3] Condoleeza Rice, former US Secretary of State had observed that relations with Japan, South Korea and India are important for empowering these nations and creating an environment in which China is more likely to behave as a responsible rising power.[4] In other words, the American strategy for managing China is calculated to increase China's stake in the existing global system and raise the cost of misusing its power.[5] Therefore, India, on its part, should look for maximum options in its relations with China and enhance its own strategic space. While welcoming greater American presence in the Asia-Pacific region, India should steer prudently in dealing with China's on going territorial disputes with Japan and South-East Asian countries.

The strategic culture of both India and China are similar in the sense that both are keen to assume great power roles they believe to be their historical or civilizational destiny. To a large extent, this is at the root of their competitive national security posture. Though both have attained regional power status, China has moved far ahead of India in the race. There is visible asymmetry between the two countries in global status and power and China will resist any attempt by India to achieve strategic parity. The mutual rivalry between the two countries is gradually acquiring maritime dimension. China has been investing heavily in securing bases and port facilities in Seychelles, Myanmar, and Pakistan so that its naval reach could extend to the Arabian Sea and the western part of the Indian Ocean where the interests of the two powers are likely to intersect in the future. However, Chinese plans to project influence beyond the South China Sea may not materialize any time soon because its naval build up has still a long way to go. It has to build a larger and sophisticated Blue Water fleet before it can effectively expand its naval might in the Indian Ocean.

China has significantly developed its military capability and infrastructure in Tibet, whereas India has only recently realized the need for strengthening road network and military capability on our side of the LAC. India needs to have the logistical capability or the infrastructure to match China in a military conflict across the LAC. China's military modernization has clear implications for India's defence planners. During most of the last two decades, its defence budget had double digit increases. China plans to spend US $142 billion for its military in 2015. The actual expenditure will be around US $200 billion because official figures do not show money spent on research and development, arms procurement, strategici rocket programmes, and so on. By comparison, India's defence spending of nearly US $50 billion seems meagre. China is already miles ahead of India in all configurations of military power. As far as nuclear and ballistic missiles are concerned, China is in a different league altogether.

India's distrust of China is based on China's track record. China violated international treaties and norms in supplying Pakistan with nuclear weapon designs, enrichment know-how, and missile capabilities. The nuclear nexus continues till this day. But while India fights shy of telling China about its concerns, the Chinese keep lecturing their Indian counterparts about the Dalai Lama, Arunachal Pradesh, and nuclear non-proliferation. Indian leaders often go out of their way to reassure China that India would not be a part of any US-led attempt to contain China, while the latter continues to undermine Indian influence in Nepal, intrudes into Bhutan and threatens our access to the 'chicken's neck' in the North East. China has been making unconcealed efforts to gain foothold in Myanmar, Bangladesh, Srilanka, and Nepal. It opposes India's membership of the UN Security Council and seeks to exclude us from regional groupings in South-East and East Asia. Chinese officials have been openly critical about US-India Nuclear Agreement and have done their level best to prevent the Nuclear Suppliers Group from supporting US-sponsored moves in favour of India. For quite sometime now, the Chinese Embassy in New Delhi has been issuing visas to applicants from Jammu & Kashmir on a separate piece of paper instead of stamping them on Indian passports, implying thereby that the state is not a part of India. The Chinese Embassy in India refuses to grant visas to residents of Arunachal State, which they deem to be Chinese territiory. New Delhi is also concerned about various reports about China's plans to build a dam across the upper reaches of the Yarlung Tsangpo (Brahmaputra River) as part of the Nagmu hydroelectric project which will have serious environmental and economic consequences for Assam. Since 2008, developments in Sino-Indian relations have been marked more by acrimony than by cooperation. There is noticeable assertiveness in the Chinese attitude, repeatedly articulated through published articles in state and party-controlled media with derogatory and threatening references to India from time to time. These developments understandably disturb security and strategic analysts in India.

China has consistently displayed aggressive nationalism in the past. It has used military power on several occasions to settle territorial disputes. This xenophobic nationalism is rooted, in the words of David Shambaugh, 'in the century of shame and humiliation foisted upon the people of China by European colonial powers, American missionaries and Japanese invaders'. Decades of indoctrination of ideas have reinforced and strengthened these societal beliefs.[6] Consequently, China tends to show no flexibility on territorial issues like Taiwan, Tibet, or the so-called British-imposed Line of Actual Control (LAC) separating China and India. The same inflexibility marks China's attitude in respect of the disputed South China Sea islands and the Diaoyu islands vis-à-vis Japan. China has used force to seize islands in the disputed South China Seas and threatened to use force in the Taiwan straits. It has attacked India and Vietnam to 'teach lessons'. Therefore, as China becomes more powerful, its neighbours feel more uncomfortable. Even if a confident, prosperous China may not turn out to be militarily aggressive, it will dominate the region through its coercive presence once it acquires the capability to project significant naval and air power far away from its territory. For the small and middle powers of Asia, constructive engagement with China seems to be the best option today. But there will be search for long term multilateral security involving other players, notably the US, Japan and India.

There is a belief in some quarters that booming bilateral trade and economic interaction will preclude armed conflict between China and India. The volume of bilateral trade has grown at an amazingly fast pace from US $2 billion in 1998 to US $70 billion in 2014. China is India's largest trading partner today. There are several other positive elements in bilateral relations like sustained, high-level exchanges and people-to-people contacts. However, there is no necessary correlation between economic interdependence and diplomatic harmony when perceived national interests are involved. The unresolved boundary dispute is at the root of the troubled history of Sino-Indian relations. Although, barring some temporary tension in one sector, the border has for the most part remained tranquil, China periodically reminds India that it is in illegal occupation of 90,000 square kilometers of 'Chinese' territory and frequently intrudes into our side of the 4057 km long LAC. The deep intrusion into the Depsang area in Ladakh on 15 April 2013, before the visit of the Chinese premier, vividly illustrates China's game plan to keep the issue alive, reiterate its claim, and test India's response and military preparedness at frequent intervals. Given the impasse, it is unrealistic to expect that this contentious issue will be resolved soon. It would take a fairly long period of time to find a fair, reasonable, and mutually acceptable solution. An unsettled border provides China the strategic leverage to keep India uncertain and nervous about Chinese intentions and capabilities. Beijing, according to some scholars, is unlikely to give up its bargaining chip until and unless it succeeds in pacifying and totally sinicizing Tibet as it has in Inner Mongolia.[7] Eighteen rounds of border talks between Special Representatives have so far failed to achieve any tangible progress in resolving the dispute. From India's point of view, too, any settlement of the dispute involving possible territorial concession would need a consensus within and outside the Indian

Parliament. This is likely to prove a major stumbling block. But, all said and done, contrary to the fears of some, China does not seem likely to opt for a war against India for recovering China's 'lost territory' across the LAC. It will carefully assess the relative military capabilities of both countries and will desist from launching an attack unless it is one hundred per cent sure of success. The aggression of 1962 was a different story altogether. Besides, there are good reasons to believe that the focus of China's new leaders will remain mainly on pressing domestic issues and watching the United States which has announced its intention to get involved in the Asia Pacific region in a big way. Nevertheless, our defence planning must always be based on the worst-case scenario. There is urgent need to speed up long-neglected infrastructure building and militarily preparededness so that we are never caught off-guard as in 1962. During his visit to China, in May 2015, the Indian Prime Minister has flagged India's concerns vis-a-vis China in very clear terms. He has said that improvement in bilateral relations depend upon resolution of the border dispute.

For many in India and elsewhere, comparing and contrasting India with China has become a fashionable pastime. Both countries are positioned at the strategic cross roads of the world. India has to live with its large neighbour and learn to manage the complex relations, which are marked by deep mutual suspicion. If India realizes its full economic and military potential, it can hope to acquire countervailing power of sorts vis-à-vis China by the end of this decade. In the coming years, India will have to watch China not only across the Himalayas but also in the larger Asian context as well as in the Indian Ocean Region, where the two countries may bump into each other because global energy needs are expected to rise by nearly 50 percent between now and 2030 and almost half of it will come from India and China alone. Both these countries will be concerned about protecting their interests throughout this region.[8] Internally, the two countries face almost identical macro-economic challenges. But China's authoritarian one-party political system is better suited to tackling these problems. India's chaotic multi-party democracy, with its persistent crisis of governance, may delay India's rapid rise as a regional power. Furthermore, India faces serious threats from within. Unlike China, threats to internal security from non-state actors such as trans-border terrorist groups, religious fundamentalists, ethnic insurgents, and maoist extremists have overshadowed traditional external military and territorial threats. These problems have assumed critical dimensions because, in more than 66 years after Independence, the Indian sovereign state has failed to deliver social and economic justice to millions of its citizens resulting in alienation amongst vast segments of its population. This has provided opportunity to hostile neighbours to manipulate vulnerable sections within society and create trouble and instability. China's strategy to encircle India and keep it boxed within the South Asia region may eventually succeed if India fails to govern itself during the remaining years of this decade and fails to resolve the multifarious threats to its internal security and and cohesion.

REFERENCES

1. Harding, Harry, 'Political Development in Post Mao China', in *Modernizing China*, Johns Hopkins University, 1986.
2. Saran, Shyam, 'Xi Jingping's Deng moment', *Business Standard*, 19 November 2013.

3. Nye Jr., Joseph, 'Work with China, Don't Contain It', 25 January 2013, Cambridge, Mass.
4. Speech by Condoleeza Rice, Tokyo, 19 March 2005.
5. Tellis, Ashley J., Carnegie Endowment for International Peace, Report dated 22 January 2014.
6. Shambaugh, David, *The New York Times*, 5 May 2008.
7. Malik, Mohan, *China and India – Great Power Rivals*, First Forum Press, 2011, p. 25.
8. Kaplan, Robert, 'Centre Stage for 21st Century', *Foreign Affairs*, March-April 2009.

3

Reconstruction of National Security Architecture

A.K. Verma

A Task Force, comprising retired seniors and heads of all government departments having national security responsibilities, with the convener of the National Security Advisory Board as its Chairman, has been holding sessions to review the existing systems and to suggest improvements, changes, and modifications of the processes, procedures, and practices, in order to bring about a qualitative change in the internal and external national security posture of the country. This Task Force is also expected to examine what remains to be done with respect to the recommendations of the task force set up after the Kargil war.

The Task Force faces a daunting task. Ensuring comprehensive security is getting more and more complex every day. The external environment has become vitiated by new perspectives of political permissiveness, which have brought in their wake questionable doctrines of unilateralism, pre-emptive strike, and regime change. Globalization has made economic penetration a much simpler activity.

Technological advances render territorial frontiers

insignificant. The emergence of a single superpower after the Soviet Union's disintegration has not resolved the equation of balance of power. Three emergent powers in Asia, China, Japan, and India, are engaged in aggressive competition for status, markets, and resources. China, in addition, is involved in a hectic pursuit of military power, to equal that of the US, in the coming decades. The world security architecture remains, therefore, in a constant flux, with new alignments, realignments, and conflicts surfacing in dramatic ways.

This growing complexity is compounded by issues of water and land, resulting in migration, refugees, and demands for more dam constructions, thus potentially creating new areas of conflict.

Threats are arising also from the appearance of newer forces operating worldwide. The concept of absolute sovereignty is no longer sacrosanct. Nations are willingly surrendering a part of their sovereignty to a larger grouping (as in the European Union), in search of greater national security. Some nations are now claiming a right to interfere in a country's affairs on the ground that events within the country are affecting their interests. Libya is an example of how its internal human rights scenario paved the way for external intervention, thus forcing a regime change.

Free movements of unstoppable ideas are of deep concern to many nations, though democracies need not fear such intrusions. Closed societies are, however, at risk. The demise of the Soviet Union owed much to the dissemination of concepts relating to democracy, human rights, and freedom of conscience by the West through Radio Liberty and Radio Free Europe. The advent of Arab Spring is also attributable to this phenomenon.

In this context, the influence of social media like the

Internet, Facebook and Twitter has to be recognized. The Arab Spring owes a lot to the facilities provided by their instantaneous communication abilities. The same methodologies come in handy for cybercrimes and cyber wars, and even the most technologically advanced nations cannot ensure total immunity for themselves.

The competition for resources and markets, already mentioned, if it becomes cutthroat, can be another source of destabilizatlon. The Soviet Union had finally lost out because its economy could not keep pace with the demands of its military, which wanted to match the West.

The rise and rise and rise of political Islam is perhaps potentially the most troublesome phenomenon of today's world. Political Islam accepts no compromise and is successfully encroaching on new ground all the while. In Europe as well as in Australia, multiculturalism has all but been declared to be a failed exercise. The line dividing political Islam from Islam is a very thin one. In all countries experiencing an Arab Spring, Islamists and non-secularists are coming to the fore. Even in Turkey, the almost century-old Ataturkian model of secular governance, is doddering. Nobody can say today with certainty what will be the shape of its future development. Some, of course, are keeping their fingers crossed, wondering if Samuel Huntington's dire predictions about civilizational clashes will come about.

Keeping a watch over such a vast spectrum of forces, developments and possible threats has now become a national security imperative. Will the Task Force be taking an objective view on steps that must be taken or be constrained by the narrow compulsions of the Executive to retain absolute executive powers in its hands over intelligence and investigative agencies?

The present national security support systems have

proved quite inadequate as several episodes repeatedly have demonstrated. There have been instances of zero intelligence, inadequate intelligence, inaccurate intelligence, miserable coordination, and poor analysis. To set the systems right and to upgrade the quality of products and performance, a set of minimum reforms are necessary. In this context, the following need to be considered.

The intelligence and investigative agencies in the West have been armed with legislative backing. This blocks unwarranted executive control and interference from outside sources and ensures administrative and operational autonomy to the agencies to pursue their own line of thought in investigation and intelligence work.

Covert operations are important operational but optional tools for intelligence work, which are available to agencies in many democracies but not in ours. Covert action covers a range of activities such as destabilization or a coup in another country, training of rebels and guerillas, financing of foreign political groups, subversion of foreign media, black propaganda, and even kidnapping or assassination. It is self-evident that all such activities cannot be legally carried out merely on the strength of an executive directive from the highest in the land. In the US, the National Security Act of 1947 vests the President of the US with discretion to order any such measure for the security of the nation, including assassination, and the CIA, as the executing agency, is duty-bound to carry out the orders. No legal action can be taken in the US against the CIA's operatives for such activity.

The option for covert action should be available to Indian agencies also. But such an option has to came with legal immunity. This reinforces the argument for giving the Indian agencies a legal basis for their existence.

The laws should provide the freedom to the agencies to devise their own systems and methodology for recruitment of their personnel. Collection of humint (intelligence through human sources) is not child's play. It tests the resourcefulness, skills, and dedication of an intelligence officer. Humint penetration is a difficult task anytime. It becomes all the more difficult when the target is a non-state adversary, such as resistance or terrorist groups like the Indian Mujahedeen operating in India.

Recruitment to intelligence services requires the scales of enrolment be set up very high, much above the standards of ordinary recruitment. It will be evident that to recruit a higher caliber of individual, the compensation packages to be offered will have to be matching.

Unfortunately, in our country, there is a basic reluctance to accept this reality. The result is that no recruitment has taken place for the junior-most direct entry into the Research and Analysis Service of the Research & Analysis Wing (RAW) for the last several years. No wonder there are complaints that RAW is not pulling its weight. In the Intelligence Bureau, an earmarking scheme had been in operation for several years from 1955. Under this scheme, the top four or five selected for the IPS each year by the UPSC would get earmarked for the IB, for the span of their entire career. This scheme enabled the IB to develop a very strong cadre of deeply motivated young officers. However, the scheme was given up when others protested that they did not have a corresponding benefit. Sadly, the IB lost out to service jealousies.

Such jealousies do arise among agencies also, leading to turf battles, poor coordination, and even non-cooperation. It would be advisable for the Task Force to look closely into this phenomenon, to delineate respective jurisdictions in very clear terms, and to prevent one from straying into the field of another.

The role of National Technical Research Organization (NTRO), created on the recommendations of the Kargil Task Force, also needs to be clearly set out. Many turf disagreements have prevented this organization from reaching its potential. Whether NTRO should remain totally independent or be brought under another overreaching entity is a question worthy of a deep scrutiny. The need to avoid duplication must be kept in mind.

Two other major issues confronting the Task Force would be the reluctance of the states to carry out police reforms as mandated by the Supreme Court and the conflicting postures on the creation of the post of a Chief of Defense Staff (CDS).

Police reforms are not seeing the light of the day simply because the states are unwilling to let police administration go out of their clutches. Pliant and subordinate police machinery becomes an effective tool for management of diverse political and party interests, whereas an independent police will be inclined to place duty above favour. The roots of the problem go back to the Police Act of 1861, which made the police subservient to the Raj and its officers. Unless this subordination is removed by another law, the situation is hardly likely to improve.

The issue of CDS is shrouded in mutual reservations of the civil and the military and fears about loss of turf within the military itself. The issue has defied resolution over the past several years. This question in all probability may, therefore, be left to linger in limbo for some more time.

On all other major matters, the Task Force has an admirable opportunity to create history by recommending the establishment of an autonomous, independent national security architecture. It owes it to the nation to do so.

4

Sino-Indian Perspectives: Emerging Roles

B.S. Das

Arrogance is not a part of subtle diplomacy. Nor does it work out as a dividend beyond a point. History speaks of several minor and major episodes which hurt the very fundamentals of exercising effective power.

Starting small, Churchill, one of the most arrogant of world leaders, lost power after winning World War II for the United Kingdom and its allies, arrogance being one of the reasons. Hitler reaching uncontrolled heights in German arrogance could not sustain his vision and was annihilated. Mao's Cultural Revolution spelt disaster for China's emerging superpower role. The Soviet Union disintegrated with Stalin's exercise of uncontrolled power and communist ideology proved to be a poor substitute for people's power. Vietnam, Iraq and Afghanistan were American follies of arrogance of power leading to a major setback to USA's pre-eminence.

One had hoped China's new leadership, a futuristic lineage, would contribute toward a new, stable, and peaceful global order. But China's arrogance, born out of a new economic surge and misplaced nationalistic fervor based on humanistic superiority and dominance, weakened its flanks with issues like the South China Sea affecting its maritime neighbors. The huge reserves, a flourishing economy, and tremendous advances in military power did not subdue Tibetan and Sinkiang outpourings. Above all, its own socioeconomic problems affecting the new generation could not be handled effectively.

China's recent intrusions into Ladakh reflects its arrogance of power, particularly, in the face of India not only being recognized as an emerging global presence but also being a close neighbour, whose stability as the second largest population of the world would affect China one way or the other. That major powers like Australia, Japan, and Vietnam are joining hands to curb China's aggressiveness, should serve as sufficient warning to China as to the potential response of other Asian neighbours to such arragance. The fast-changing scenario In Asia, West Asia and others is bound to affect these relations further. Thus, one has to see Sino-Indian relation in a wider context.

China, emerging as a superpower and competing with the USA, cannot let India emerge as a parallel power in the Asian region. Economic growth leads to political power supported by a country's armed strength. India is emerging as a competing power, which is perceived as a threat by China. It will, therefore, exercise its leverage to levels that obstruct India's growing clout in the coming years. In China's present perception, India has to be limited to a regional role in South Asia.

Historically, China exercised power by creating tributaries in its peripheries. Tibet, never an integral part of China, paid a token tribute to the Chinese Imperial Court as a tributary. China occupied a hierarchical position, exercising suzerainty over Tibet through its resident representative located in Lhasa. The same principle was extended to territories surrounding China. Historically, the British, extending political power and consequent treaties, entered into a balancing act to contain China's political and economic power. Even military force was applied through expeditions into various territories, like Younghusband's expedition into Tibet in 1904 resulting in a treaty between the British and Tibet. The McMohan Agreement was a consequence of British suzerainty over these areas. Now, with the assertion of its power, China cannot have a parallel competing centre, while India has all the elements to emerge as just such a major power in the coming decades.

Both countries are undergoing a social revolution. China's political ideology of Communism, on which the State is based, cannot sustain this change. The Soviet Union broke apart because of its inner contradictions. Diversities in language, culture, and economic disparities eroded Communist pre-eminence in governance. The coming decades will see a radical change in the entire economic and social structure in China, which will find itself inching its way towards becoming a well-defined, multi-structural social and economic power without any constraints of ideology or other dividing factors. Nationalism will become the driving force for China.

China's efforts to weaken India through support to Pakistan or threaten areas of India's strategic interest will delay China's emergence as a competing power to the USA. India has no visions of being 'super' per se. It is only struggling to assert its rightful role in ensuring peace and security in the concerned Asian region through a powerful economic role. Yes, this does imply political pre-eminence with a strong military back up. However, there is no conflict of interest with China.

By any yardstick, a collaborative role between these Asian giants can create a new global order ensuring peace, territorial integrity, and a very progressive economic region, removing imbalances as they exist in the long run. Tri-polar competition is emerging, with USA, China, and India, and India as the supportive structure in a highly advanced and developed social order with few conflicts. One can hope to see this by 2050. It is not an idealistic hope but rather an inevitably compulsive one. The world will have to move in that direction.

Chinese pragmatism is bound to adjust to Indian sensitivities. The role of either cannot be subverted beyond a point. As we move into the next decade, this realization will be forced through increasing scientific challenges and environmental changes. Ideology will be replaced by pragmatism.

The present pressure tactics of China on India has to be seen in a broader perspective. Post-1949, when the Communists took over China, they started the process of consolidating their power. Apart from serious boundary problems with the Soviet Union, the ideological premise of supremacy over Lenin's Communism was Mao's key approach to China power. The Soviet Union, asserting its benign guidance to international Communism, which included China, was resented by Mao, who considered the Soviets to be pseudo-Communists. Soviet economic and arms assistance failed to win over China, which designed its own strategy of global ideological dominance. When India inched its way closer to the Soviet Union, it was perceived to be a long term threat to China's interests.

China felt its flanks being weakened with American presence in the region. The Sino-Indian war of 1962 was part of a consequence of this thinking. India was too weak and could be subdued. Also, it posed a threat to China's interests in Tibet. Historically, China had laid claims to large areas in the Himalayan belt in which India figured prominently. China, capturing Aksai Chin to protect its western flank adjoining Sinkiang and Tibet, was the first assertion of its power. It entered Arunachal to establish its claim, but withdrew voluntarily to a line which is now the line of actual control. Nothing prevented China from occupying Arunachal if it had wanted to. To claim it as a part of Tibet is a bargaining strategy that China uses as a pressure point, especially in recent times.

If one were to analyse China's frequent incursions into India's northeastern region, inclusive of Bhutan and Sikkim, what emerges is that they believe to be entering territories they have already claimed. That their claim is not accepted by India does not deter them. These were claim lines of China but not accepted. There are innumerable cases of Chinese intrusions, military and otherwise, in the so-called claimed territories. But, there is hardly any instance where they intruded to stay. In Bhutan, Chinese troops frequently entered the territory and stayed for hours. But they always went back.

China is a pragmatic State, superb in the art of dramatizing event and pressurizing India, especially on boundary claims. However, it plays its game with the clear objective of making India uncomfortable. It would not be wrong in assuming that China's subtle pressures are meant to keep India confined to the status of a South Asian power. In this direction, China's friendship with Pakistan is an act of balancing India and preventing it from going beyond its presumed role of a regional power. The added element of this strategy is China's major apprehension about USA's closeness to India. It has a larger perception of India being used as a balancing power to China's emerging status. If one views this situation objectively, India is the only country, which, by virtue of it's political, economic, and defense content, could effectively deter China's ambitions.

China is facing enormous socio-economic problems in its polity, in spite of a stupendous economic growth. The strains that are emerging cannot be resolved by a depleting ideology. The entire spectrum of Chinese Communism, which sustained China's stability, is changing, in the light of the common man's increasing needs and demands. The ethnic conflicts, in spite of China's 90 per cent Han content, are becoming unmanageable, mostly because the leverage of power and control does not permit free expression or participation. The People's Liberation Army (PLA), the centre of China's ideological support and power, is emerging as the most important vehicle of China's global role.

One should not be unduly perturbed by China (notwithstanding its tactics of pressures on India) or with Pakistan. India, as it emerges, cannot be substituted by Pakistan in China's collaborative role strategy. In spite of being poorly governed, India will still be of great strategic value to both China and the USA. In the hypothetical instance of China and India reaching the bargaining table, the final round will indeed witness Aksai Chin remaining a part of China and we must accept it. Let us accept the fact that Aksai Chin will remain a part of China, in the final round of bargaining between India and China. Ground realities will have to be taken into account by both sides. If India is weakened by China with Pakistan's assistance, a distant possibility, it will be damaging to China's own ambition to be a superpower in this region and beyond. Our efforts should be to evolve a strategy of collaboration with China, conducive to India's new role.

It does not serve China's interests to occupy Arunachal and go to war with India. The rest of the boundary is negotiable, keeping even Pakistan's interests in mind. Future wars will not be conventional. The missile is the accepted norm of the weapon of future wars. American experience in Iraq, and now in Afghanistan, is a pointer. Kargil failed. Though we should not be complacent, India is entering a new phase of weaponry, which could be devastating.

Nevertheless, China is not preparing to invade India. Its new roads, railways, airports are all part of a larger strategic plan of easy access to pressurize as well use these assets as part of its economic dominance, a weapon of greater value and effectiveness. India needs to learn this effective strategy to play a major role as a power of great significance.

As for nuclear deterrence, it is a misnomer. Mao once told the Russians that China would survive a nuclear attack because of its large population and depth. A strange logic which proved only one point: a nuclear attack is self-destructive. No nation can afford to be destroyed. This is nuclear deterrence. Rajiv Gandhi realized the significance of this and attempted to pave an acceptable way. He failed, but is remembered for his significant contribution in highlighting 'deterrence' in the correct perspective. One witnessed this in 1962 in Moscow, in the Cuban context, when the Soviets withdrew their nuclear missile.

China understands this game fairly well. Apart from building its own nuclear strength as a balance in the bigger power game, it played a role in North Korea and Pakistan to not only balance American and Indian interests in the Asian region, but also swing it to its advantage in the new equations that are emerging. China's nationalistic fervor, with Han domination, is a weapon that it uses effectively. India has no such matching levers. Its tremendous diversity and spontaneous verbosity are well understood. Despite these shortcomings of India, China cannot emerge as a superpower without India's effective collaborative role. In this part of the world, India matters and China knows it. It therefore, plays a game of keeping India on its toes with one arm for peace, and the other for pressures.

Recent events in the South China Sea and concerned countries at loggerhead with China, especially Japan, are taking a new direction towards the containment of China as a superpower. Both Tibet and Sinkiang remain flashpoints. China also cannot ignore the possibilities of an Indo-Pak détente in the coming years. With India's improved relations with Myanmar and Bangladesh, a new economic power centre is emerging. Japan and Australia seeking closer links with India with a maritime security extending from the Indian to the Pacific Oceans cannot be ignored by China.

The way the world is moving, this is the most significant transition to a new order taking shape by 2050. If India plays its cards with confidence and understanding of the emerging scenario, it will emerge as a power of consequence. The prophecy of a three-pillar world order, with the USA, China, and India as key players, is based on the above assumptions.

Taking the Indo-Pak scenario into account and India's emerging political role, there is no way Pakistan can resolve the Kashmir issue without India's concurrence and active participation. Musharraf realized this and was working on a pragmatic solution. Recent public postures on the Kashmir issue by Nawaz Sharif at various forums are strategies to keep the army and the Taliban on leash. He knows the ground realities of keeping the talks with India going. Sharif also knows well that China, itself, will never go to war with

India, especially with Aksai Chin as a major factor.

Both China and India are well aware of the ground realities. A permanent settlement with India will be based on that. In short, with minor adjustments, the de facto situation will translate itself into re-definition of the borders. The Simla Agreement of 1971 laid its foundations. India cannot be dislodged from its existing geographical control, nor can India throw out the Chinese or Pakistanis from the occupied areas. This will not be achieved in a hurry but must happen in the interest of the three countries in the coming years. Economic interaction and political strategy will make this process easier. Till then, more violence and turmoil will dominate the scene in the coming decade.

5

Police Reforms: Why This Delay?

Prakash Singh

It is one of the ironies of modern India that, while we are preparing to send a mission to the moon, while there has been a revolution in information technology, while there has been vast improvement in the rail and road networks across the country, while we have taken a quantum leap in nuclear science, while we have one of the fastest growing economies in the world, we are yet—more than sixty years after Independence—saddled with a colonial police with a feudal mindset. There have been any number of Commissions, both at the state and Central levels—State Police Commissions, National Police Commission, Gore Committee, Ribeiro Committee, Padmanabhaiah Committee, Malimath Committee, to name only a few— which made recommendations for reforms, but these received no more than cosmetic treatment at the hands of the government with the result that there has been hardly any change in the colonial policing which we inherited from the British. The common man does not feel secure or protected —on the contrary, he may be harassed or even persecuted by the police if he dares to take a stand against the establishment.

There are more than 20,000 police stations and posts across the length and breadth of the country, and their working impinges on the life of the common man from Srinagar to Kanyakumari and from Ahmedabad to Aizwal, irrespective of whether he has a complaint or not. It is a sad commentary on our Republic that we have not been able to transform the police into an instrument of service upholding the Rule of Law and inspiring confidence amongst the people.

It needs to be emphasized that police reforms are absolutely essential if India is to emerge as a great power. Economic progress cannot be sustained if we are not able generate a safe and secure environment. The democratic structure may also crumble if we do not arrest the trend of criminals gaining ascendancy in public life.

The three greatest problems confronting the country today are: the challenge of international terrorism, the spread of Maoist influence over a huge geographical area, and the cancer of corruption. If we are to tackle these problems effectively, there is no getting away from having a professional police force, well trained and equipped, highly motivated, and committed to upholding the laws of the land and the Constitution of the country. The police are the first responders in the event of any terrorist attack or Maoist violence, and they are also the backbone of our intelligence, investigation, and anti-corruption agencies.

Supreme Court's Directions

On 22 September, 2006, the Supreme Court gave a historic judgement on police reforms containing seven directions, out of which six were meant for the state governments/ Union Territories and one for the Union Government. It directed the setting up of three institutions, namely:

a) the State Security Commission, which would lay down the broad policies and give directions for the performance of the preventive tasks and service-oriented functions of the police;

b) the Police Establishment Board, comprising the Director General of Police and four other senior officers of the Department who would decide transfers, postings, promotions, and other service-related matters of departmental officers and others; and

c) the Police Complaints Authority, at the district and state levels, with a view to inquiring into allegations of serious misconduct by police personnel.

Besides, this Court ordered that the Director General of Police should be selected by the state government from amongst the three senior-most officers of the Department, who have been empanelled for promotion to that rank by the UPSC, and that he shall have a prescribed minimum tenure of two years. Police officers on operational duties in the field like the IG Zone, DIG Range, SP Incharge of District, and SHO Incharge of Police Station would also have a minimum tenure of two years.

The Court also ordered separation of the investigating police from the law and order police to ensure speedier investigation, better expertise, and improved rapport with the people.

The Union Government was asked to set up a National Security Commission for the selection and placement of heads of Central Police Organizations, upgrading the effectiveness of these forces and improving the service conditions of its personnel.

The aforesaid orders were to be implemented by the end of 2006. The time limit was subsequently extended till 31 March, 2007. Fifteen states have passed Bills/Acts, but unfortunately, these are not in keeping with the letter and spirit of the Court's directions. Actually, these were passed to circumvent the implementation of the Supreme Court's directions. The other states have been dragging their feet in the matter. The Thomas Committee, which was appointed by the Supreme Court to monitor the implementation of its directions, expressed 'dismay over the total indifference to the issue of reforms in the functioning of Police being exhibited by the States' in its report dated 23 August, 2010.

The Justice Verma Committee, which was constituted to examine the Amendments to Criminal Law in the context of a gangrape incident, which happened in Delhi on 16 December, 2012, deplored: 'The Supreme Court's judgement of 2006 in *Prakash Singh*'s case giving certain directions for the autonomy and improving the quality of the police force remain to be implemented by all the governments. Action in this behalf does not brook any further delay.'

The Committee urged 'all states to fully comply with all six Supreme Court directives in order to tackle systemic problems in policing which exist today.' It went on to say: 'We believe that if the Supreme Court's directions in *Prakash Singh* are implemented, there will be a crucial modernization of the police to be service oriented for the citizenry in a manner which is efficient, scientific, and consistent with human dignity.'

The present position may be summarized as below:

(a) The Supreme Court issued seven directions on Police Reforms in 2006. Out of these, six were meant for the state governments and one for the Central Government.

(b) Fifteen states have passed Police Acts which do not conform to the letter and spirit of the Supreme Court's directions

(c) The remaining state governments have submitted affidavits of partial compliance. However, even these are not reflected at the ground level.
(d) The Central government has yet to pass the Delhi Police Bill.

The Government of India should, without any further delay, pass a central legislation on the subject along the lines of the Model Police Act drafted by the Soli Sorabjee Committee, incorporating therein the directions of the Supreme Court. The government should pursuade the state governments to either implement the mandatory directions of the Supreme Court or pass laws under Article 252 of the Constitution along the lines of the central legislation on the subject.

The Supreme Court's directions, it needs to be emphasized, are not for the glory of the police; they exist to give better security and protection to the people of the country, to uphold their human rights, and generally improve governance. If sincerely implemented, they would have far reaching implications and would change the working philosophy of the police. The 'ruler's police' would be transformed into a 'people's police'.

Other Relevant Aspects of Police Reforms

Apart from the core areas identified by the Supreme Court, reforms are urgently required in some other fields also:

Manpower

The police-population ratio in India in 2012, according to the Bureau of Police Research and Development (BPR&D), was 1:551 (as against 1:334 in USA, 1:290 in UK, and 1:416 in New Zealand). It works out to 181 personnel per lakh of population and compares unfavourably with the international medien figure of 303 (as per the UNODC statistics of 2010). What is worse, there are huge vacancies in several states. According to BPR&D, the actual strength of the police force was 16,60,666 against the sanctioned strength 22,09,027. The vacancies need to be filled up so that the police-population ratio improves and comes close to international standards.

Infrastructure

There are deficiencies in motor transport, communications, and forensic support. According to the figures available, the police have slightly less than seven vehicles per 100 policemen. Communication-wise, there are 350 police stations in the country with no telephone, 107 without wireless, and 38 police stations with neither telephone nor wireless. Forensic support is poor and 5,61,914 exhibits were pending examination on 01 January, 2012. There should be forensic laboratories at the Divisional/Range levels, if not in every district.

Housing

Housing facilities have a direct bearing on the morale of the personnel. These facilities are quite inadequate. The government is committed to providing accommodation to all the police personnel, but at present, we have only 5.40 lakh family accommodations for 16.40 lakh police personnel. Housing facilities require substantial augmentation.

Training

Training remains a neglected area. As recommended by the Second Administrative Reforms Commission, the deputation to training institutions must be made more attractive in terms of facilities and allowances so that the best talent is drawn as instructors. Besides, training should focus on bringing attitudinal change in the police in order that they are more sensitive to citizens' needs.

Modernization

Modernization of police forces should get high priority. The Comptroller and Auditor General has, in a recent report, revealed that progress in enhancing the mobility of the police and giving it sophisticated weapons and other equipment has been tardy. The process must be accelerated. Government of India has approved a modernization plan for the period 2013–14 to 2016–17. The states should finalize their action plans and submit the same to the MHA at the earliest. Priority should be given to: cyber security, counter terrorism/insurgency, training and the use of technology in various aspects of policing.

Registration of Crime

This is a very sore point with the people. There is concealment and minimization of crime on a big scale. To a large extent, politicians are responsible for it. In the State of Uttar Pradesh (UP), for example, directions were given by the state government that crime figures be brought down by 70 per cent, and quite a few senior officers, who could not execute this *firman* were placed under suspension. Opposition parties also raise a hue and cry to tarnish the image of the government if crime figures show an increase. Society, as a whole, should accept the inevitability of increase in crime with every passing year.

Conclusion

Whatever be the priority of the government—security of the common man, survival of democracy, maintaining the trajectory of economic progress, or dealing with the major threats confronting the country—there is no getting away from the inescapable conclusion that we must have a reformed, restructured, and revitalized police force.

Police reforms are much too urgent to be delayed and much too important to be neglected any longer. A professional police, accountable to the people of the country and placing the highest importance to upholding the Rule of Law, will provide the essential foundation for a progressive, modern India, taking its rightful place in the comity of nations.

6

Pakistan Army: A Divided Army with the Mask of Unity and History of Unsuccessful Coups

S.K. Datta

Chief Justice Munir, in a landmark judgment in 1958, opened the floodgate of successful and unsuccessful coups in Pakistan. Zulfikar Ali Bhutto, from his condemned cell, described Pakistan as Coupistan. The judiciary, instead of protecting and sustaining democracy in Pakistan, bent down before the army generals, may be out of fear of being sacked and victimized or to earn favour. Whatever it may be, the judiciary not only failed to protect democracy, but paved the way for subsequent subversion of democracy in Pakistan.

Pakistan has earned the reputation of building up two industries—those of rumours and conspiracies. On the rumour 'industry', there was a popular joke in Pakistan during Ayub's regime: Ayub told his son, 'There are many rumour factories these days in Karachi producing all sorts of propaganda against me', and his son, who became an industrialist after leaving the army replied: 'Daddy, do you think I should buy these too', (Mushahid Hussain, *Pakistan Politics*, p. 27).

Mushahid Hussain writes that Pakistanis are avid believers of conspiracy theories. And why not, particularly, when people have seen almost all the regimes in Pakistan, right from its inception, undergoing change through conspiracy. Each successful coup was staged with a brigade strength of force by a serving Chief of the Army Staff, aided by selected 'stallions' from Rawalpindi Army Headquarters.

In Pakistan, there were four successful army coups from Oen Ayub to Gen Musharraf. Gen Yahya's taking over the reigns from Ayub was a coup of a sort. These apart, there were four other recorded unsuccessful army coup attempts. They, too, need to be discussed to highlight the fragility and vulnerability of the system. The much talked about unity at the corps commander level is just a manifestation of a deep desire to perpetuate army rule directly or indirectly. It is realized at the highest level that any division or groupism in the army would mean reduction of the army's status in Pakistan. This is the binding factor of the so-called unity in the Pakistan army.

The army eats up 32 per cent of the total budget which is around eight per cent of the country's GDP. This is money that could have been used for the development of the economy, health care, education, safe drinking water, et cetera. The perks available to serving and retired army officers are unthinkable in any developed or developing country. Apart from a few, most of them live in royal style, owning more than one house and reluctant to sacrifice all these perks. An institution called the Fouji Foundation takes care of the financial interests of retired officers. This and other unreasonable benefits can be sustained only by a facade of the apparent unity of the Pakistan Army.

From perks to corruption is a short journey. As defence is out of the bounds of civil administration, there are many allegations of corruption in defence deals with kickback culture. They are rarely investigated for fear of reprisal from the defence services. Musharraf, after capturing power to obtain public support, appointed an Accountability Bureau under Gen Amjad, only to investigate cases against civil servants and politicians. Under intense public pressure, Musharraf belatedly allowed 20 defence-related cases to the Accountability Bureau and poor Gen Amjad was shifted to slow down the process. Gen Amjad was reputed for his integrity in Pakistan Army.

Such cases of misuse of power are not rare in other developing countries. Even in India, such allegations are made, but because of democratic functioning, either institutional or public pressure is built up for inquiry or investigation. All these are lacking in Pakistan because of the army's constant interference in running the government and controlling all organs of the State.

The failed army coups deserve a deeper study to know the psyche of the junior officers, who led such coups. How is it that the myth of unity in the Pakistan army has been sustained far too long? Diverse interests are at play and the army reflects the chaotic situation of the country with sectarian clashes, religious fundamentalism, ethnic conflicts, and inter-provincial disharmony that are never resolved. They haunt Pakistan. Moreover, the Pakistani army is perceived as a provincial army of Punjab.

1951 Abortive Rawalpindi Conspiracy Case

Maj Gen Akbar Khan, as Chief of the General Staff (CGS) under the Commander-in-Chief of of Gen Ayub Khan, tried an abortive coup in 1951. He had leftist leanings then, an unusual position, as Generals in Pakistan are usually Rightist and not Leftist. He was the same gentleman, who had organized a tribal raid in Kashmir and assumed the name of a Muslim conqueror, Tariq. In fact, he did the raid on instructions from Liaquat Ali Khan. He got an idea of a coup against his own mentor Liaquat Ali Khan. He discussed the idea with a coterie of his favorite officers, but the plan could not be implemented as he was sent to London, for a course. In London, he reportedly got in touch with Left-wing leaders. Upon his return to Pakistan, he was made CGS, a very important position in the Pakistani army. He revised his plan of conspiracy for the ouster of the civilian government in favour of a pro-Soviet regime.

Born in 1912 in Peshawar, Akbar Khan joined the army and also graduated from Sandhurst in 1933. Ayub was also a Sandhurst graduate. In 1947, Akbar Khan was a Colonel in the Pakistani army. Before that, he as part of the Indian army had shown bravery fighting the Japanese in Burma. He was a Brigadier when he had organized the tribal raid in Kashmir.

The conspiracy documents were kept secret and were unlocked in 1955 by the PPP government. Hasan Zaheer, on the basis of these documents, had written a book: *The Times and Trials of the Rawalpindi Conspiracy Case 1951* (Oxford). Akbar Khan was described by the author as an unbalanced personality with cruelty and rashness as his trademarks. Zaheer quotes a source pointing to clinical madness that ran in Akbar's Umanzai tribe. His first marriage produced two abnormal children. One was a spastic. His thinking capacity was extremely poor. His Kashmir raid was a fiasco that hurt his reputation. In support of his mad plan of war in Kashmir, he wrote a book two decades after the event, passing the buck on to others. In this book, he proposed *Jihad* for annexation of Kashmir. A contrary person, he quoted Muslim history in support of his rightist view. His political view was like a pendulum swinging from Left to Right.

Akbar managed to build up a team of officers, some with doubtful leanings. Added to this, he roped in poet Faiz Ahmed Faiz and Sajjad Zaheer, two prominent Left-wing political leaders in the conspiracy. One of the team members, Lt Col Siddique Raja, realized that the whole plan was unrealistic. He opposed the proposed coup and informed Gen Ayub. To prove the case, Siddique became an approver. In planning the conspiracy, there was no element of secrecy. Akbar even roped in Gen Azam Khan, who hated Ayub but was not made a direct conspirator. The coup failed as all the conspirators were promptly picked up and prosecuted in a general court martial (GCM). This was the first failed army coup in Pakistan. Sajjad Zaheer, who had migrated from India, returned to India for the rest of his life.

The 1973 Conspiracy Case

On 30 March 1973, 46 Armed Forces officers were arrested for their alleged attempt to overthrow Zulfikar Ali Bhutto's government, which came to power in 1971 in a dramatic manner after the dismemberment of Pakistan. Gen Chisti said that the motive of the conspiracy was to ensure the exposure of those responsible for failure of military operation in East and West Pakistan in the 1971 war and bring to book those responsible for the same. Earlier, half of these conspirators were decorated with medals like Sitara-e-Jurat for their part in the 1965 and 1971 wars against India. Two of the conspirators, according Chisti, had managed to escape from their POW camps in India by digging a long tunnel for two months which remained undetected. Taking the background of the alleged conspirators into account, Chisti doubted if they had really planned to stage a coup. 'It was more a whispering campaign than a plot.'

The case, however, rested on the allegation that Bhutto, Gen Yahya Khan, and other generals were squarely responsible for the amputation of the country. Bhutto should not have spared Gen Yahya Khan and the other generals.

Bhutto's slander campaign against the army after becoming the president, the conspirators thought it had lowered the prestige of the army. It was humiliation heaped on a defeated army.

Only 25 officers, headed by Brig F. Bali and Col Akerm Afridi, were charged in the general court martial presided over by Gen Zia-ul-Haq. One of the members of the court, Jehan Dad Khan, was promoted to Lt General subsequently. At the initial stages, he had named some of the conspirators. The conspiracy was entirely leaked out by Col Tariq Raf to the intelligence agencies. Major Saeed Malik, son of a General, who was a part of the conspiracy, told Jehan Dad Khan that, like his father, he had no patience to wait for 35 years to reach a place of honour in the army, and therefore, joined the conspiracy to elevate himself quickly.

The conspirators fixed a day in April 1973 for the proposed coup. The alleged coup was detected and the officers were arrested. Gen Zia, not Chief of the Army Staff (COAS) then, was asked to hold the court martial. It was during this period that Gen Zia secured easy access to Bhutto, as he often met him to discuss the case. A point to be noted is that it was unusual to discuss a court case with the prime minister.

Many of the conspirators were awarded life imprisonment, while others received lighter sentences varying from three years to 15 years. Gen Zia, when he came to power by staging a coup, released all the sentenced officers. By doing this, he sent out a message that the punishments awarded earlier were on the prornptings of

Bhutto. Some of the released officers went abroad; none was taken back into the army. Not much has come out in the open regarding this case.

1980 Aborted Coup d'Etat

This failed coup has a long history. There was an attempted coup in April 1976 by Maj Gen Tajammal Hussain Malik. He was considered a professional soldier. He had participated in the 1965 war and also in the 1971 war in East Pakistan. He considered himself honest and others dishonest. This was his obsession for which there was no cure. Such self-righteous people are generally suspicious of others. He suffered from a 'holier-than-thou' syndrome. India, too, has its share of such people. Added to this, he was afflicted with the 'religious bug' and dreamed of establishing a truly Islamic State in Pakistan, as he did not find enough of Islamization during Zia's rule. Such a General would most definitely be overlooked for further promotion. As he was. This trauma led him to believe that the time had come to strike. He discussed the plan with Col Aslam Zubairi, an officer from Corps of Signals. He tasked him to obtain some information. Instead, Col Zubairi promptly revealed the conspiracy to his senior officers, including Gen Zia. Maj Gen Tajammal was soon dismissed from service in 1976.

After forced retirement, Tajammal moved to Lahore and began an association with Maulana Maudoodi of Jamat-e-Islam. Maudoodi was not in a position to help Tajammal. Nevertheless, Tajammal did not stop there. He met Air Marshal Asghar Khan who, too, failed to provide any help to Tajammal. But Tajammal. joined Asghar Khan's party, Tehrik-e-Istaglal, only to leave shortly and form his own party, Islami Inqlabi, which was a one-member party. His utter frustration dominated his psyche. He hated Bhutto for not enforcing 'Nizam-e-Mustafa', and he strongly felt that Zia needed to be removed. That was in 1980.

The plan was to carry out Gen Zia's assassination during Pakistan Day Parade on 23 March, 1980, on the model of the assassination of President Anwar Sadat of Egypt. Islamaboali, an Egyptian army officer, had shot dead President Anwar Sadat when he was reviewing the army parade. In Tajammal's plan, his son Capt Naveed, was to fire at Gen Zia in the same way. Tajammal had formed a revolutionary council in advance to take over the country after Zia's assassination. Capt Naveed was in the Baluch Regiment already selected for the scheduled Pakistan Day Parade. It was a task of great magnitude to find out all those who were involved in the conspiracy, as each conspirator had taken a vow of secrecy in the name of the Holy Koran. The Inter-Services Intelligence (ISI) focused on three conspirators, namely, Tajammal, his son Naveed, and Tajammals nephew, Major Riaz.

On the D-day, all the conspirators converged at Rawalpindi. They were located by ISI's surveillance parties. Military intelligence had earlier suggested five separate parties like Look Out Party, Cordon Party, Raiding Party, Arrest Party, and Search Party to apprehend the conspirators. The ISI rejected this proposed mobilization as being unnecessarily massive for the operation at hand.

The task was entrusted to Brig Timrazi, who was incharge of the joint Counter Intelligence Bureau of the ISI. Major Riaz was first picked up by Brig Tirmazi in a dramatic way was arrested from his Lahore residence. Capt Naveed from his army tent. Thus ended the coup. If not detected on time, Gen Zia's fate would have been the same as that of President Sadat of Egypt.

1995 Failed Coup

The last failed army coup was busted on 14 October 1995, when 40 odd army officers, having links with some of the Islamic fundamentalist groups, were arrested. The highest ranking officer involved was Maj Gen Zahirul Islam Abbasi. The other conspirators arrested were one brigadier, one colonel, and other ranking officers. Maj Gen Abbasi had earlier worked in India as Pakistan's Military Attache when he was a brigadier. Because of adverse activities against the security of India, he was declared a persona-non-grata by the Indian government.

Maj Gen Abbasi belonged to the Infantry and was holding the post of Director General at GHQ Rawalpindi. He was one of the 'stallions' of Rawalpindi. This is description often used by the press in Pakistan. The conspiracy was busted by the 'heynas' that is sleuths of the Intelligence Bureau (IB) and the Military Intelligence. It may be recalled that the IB was strengthened by Benazir Bhutto as Prime Minister. She did not wish the ISI to involve itself in counter intelligence operations within Pakistan.

The object of this conspiracy was to bring about an Islamic revolution in Pakistan, as in their perception, Pakistan had not become a truly Islamic state. In addition there was an agenda for liberation of Kashmir, a pet theme of the 'stallions' of Rawalpindi and 'hynas' of ISI. It does provide an agenda for army and fundamentalist groups to sustain the so-called unity of Pakistan and its army. M.H. Ansari, a journalist of repute wrote in *Dawn* on 18 October 1995 that plotters had close links with the Hizbul Mujahideen and the Harkat-ul-Ansar, which were known for their involvement in international terrorism. The arrested conspirators wanted Pakistan to get its army involved in the so-called freedom struggle in Kashmir. It was said that the arrested officers even implicated Gen Musharraf then functioning as DG Military Operations. Zero action could be taken against him for want of evidence.

A chance arrest of an activist of Harkat-ul-Ansar at Muzzarffarabad revealed the conspiracy. The plan to open up the case was kept secret. Surveillance was mounted on the core suspects. Foolishly, Brig Mustansir Billow, an officer of the Baluch Regiment and an unamed Colonel visited the tribal areas of Western Frontier Provinces (WFP). High level officers traveling in a one-star car was insurance enough for safe passage of the truck.

These two officers were surprised when the Attock checkpost staff insisted on checking the truck following them. The Brigadier and the Colonel pleaded with the checkpost staff but to no avoil, as the checkpost staff had already been alerted by the agencies. The search yielded a cache of weapons. The duo were arrested and handed over to the military. In such operations, the sleuths give a long rope to conspirators so as to catch them with sufficient evidence for prosecution.

No one ever doubted the sincerity of the officers involved in the conspiracy. They had raised money by selling their earthly possessions. They were so sure of their plan's success that they had in advance designated senior ranks to themselves and had told their brethren in the extremists groups that a new Islamic era would be ushered in to Pakistan. A retired Lieutenent General was reportedly roped in, who agreed to play a silent role. The journalist, Kamran Khan, reported in daily 'News' on 16 October 1995 that the conspirators had close links with Lt Gen [Retd] Javed Nassir of ISI fame. While in service, he had deviated to religious fundamentalism and became an active member of Tabligi Jamaat, which became famous for recruitment *jihadis* for Afghan *jihad*. He misused ISI aircraft to reach Raiwind, the Jamaat headquarters.

Kamran Khan also reported that COAS Gen Abdul Waheed had to dismiss Lt Gen Javed Nasir for providing covert military support to Muslim rebels in about a dozen countries of the world. There were reports that he was also dismissed due to American pressure. After leaving service, Javeed Nasir became security advisor to Nawaz Sharif, who when he became the Prime Minister of Pakistan, eventually made him the President of Pakistan Sikh Gurduwara Prabhandak Committee to reorganize insurgency in India, which he attempted with the aid of some misguided Sikh expatriates living in USA and Canada.

Javeed Nasir escaped arrest in the 1995 conspiracy because of his army contacts. This bearded General has intense hatred for India and Indians. On 6 December 1995, the Lahore high court dismissed an appeal filed against the arrest of the army officers. On 31 December 1995, a court martial against four senior army officers commenced in the famous Attock Fort near Peshawar. On 30 October 1996 these officers were convicted and awarded various terms imprisonment. Much remains unknown about the fate of the other conspirators and their civilian collaborators.

The plot was amateurish in concept and execution. As stated by Gen [Retd] Faiz Ali Chisti, a successful army coup can only be led by COAS and not by junior officers in Pakistan. The reason is that even senior officers like Corps Commanders would be always haunted by a possible division in the army. A divided army in Pakistan may lead to downgrading of the role of the army in the politics of the country. In such a situation, the army wIll be totally irrelevant in the peculiar power structure of Pakistan within which it has been enjoying a privileged position both under the civilian and army rules. Therefore they have to wear the mask of unity.

Agartala Conspiracy Case

Mujibur Rehman, a leader from East Pakistan, drew strength from regional aspirations of Bengalis who formed the majority in Pakistan. The Bengalis were oppressed for seeking parity with West Pakistan, which treated East Pakistan as its colony for economic and political exploitation. The Bengalis felt totally alienated when Bhutto said on the floor of the National Assembly that, during the 1965 war, China had promised to protect East Pakistan in case of an Indian attack. Such a statement did affect the psyche of the majority of Bengalis. They realized that the integrity of Pakistan was for West Pakistan only.

After the Tashkent Declaration, Bengalis were largely happy, while West Pakistanis, mainly Punjabis, were bitter. The opposition parties held a two-day meeting on 5 and 6 February 1965 in Lahore, were the Tashkent Declaration was condemned. At this meeting, Mujib presented his famous six point programme, calling for greater autonomy for East Pakistan. It went unchallenged. Thus, Mujib could float his idea from the soil of Lahore without any visible opposition at that stage.

Ayub lost his grip after the 1965 war with India. The public bitterness, the political unrest unleashed by wily Bhutto, and the deterioration of economic conditions due to imposition of US sanctions were hitting hard. Pakistan was in a mess. In such a situation, pressures built up a theory of conspiracy. The agencies worked out a great Agartala conspiracy case against Mujibur Rehaman to defame him in the eyes of the people and prevent him from his volatile political activities.

A piece of 'intelligence' was developed when Ayub visited East Pakistan in December 1967 that an attempt would be made to blow up his plane enroute to a place called Chandragana. His visit was cancelled. It was alleged that some civil and military officials of East Pakistan were planning the secession of East Pakistan from Pakistan. To make the story believable, some Indian conspirators were also named.

As a quick follow up on January 1968, 28 persons were arrested on charges of treason. Three senior civil servants, a naval officer and a number of non-commissioned, seamen and civilians were roped in. In the history of conspiracy such a large contingent of people intent on hatching a conspiracy is unheard of. It was alleged that P.N. Ojha, the First Secretary of the Indian Deputy Commission, had supposedly met Lt Col Misra and Major Menon at Agartala to hatch the conspiracy. The Army GHQ was handling the case under the supervision of Gen Yahya Khan.

The GHQ completed its investigation and submitted a report recommending trial. It is impossible to imagine how an investigation could be conducted by the army as any criminal investigation requires a clear understanding of the law as well as the procedure of prosecution.

Gen Yahya argued that one of the conspirators was Mujibur Rehaman and that the case against him was foolproof. When the summary of the case was spelt out, Altaf Gauhar, then Ayub's Information Secretary, felt the case was based on 'assumptions' and 'speculations'. There was no material to connect Mujib with the case. During the alleged conspiracy period, most of the time Mujib was in jail. When Ayub was told of this gross inadequacy, he expressed his opinion not to prosecute Mujib. Mujib's name was deleted from the list of accused.

A special tribunal was established with three judges, serving and retired. The famous errand boy of Ayub, Manzur Qadir, agreed to lead the prosecution case. Before the opening of the trial, the name of Mujibur Rehaman was again included, as that would make the case lively and strong. 'Yahya must have known that the case would explode like a bombshell, rob the government of whatever credibility it possessed, and alienate East Pakistan, perhaps for good' [Altaf]. Ayub made a trip to London for a medical check up. The Bengalis in London organized ad demonstration in favour of Mujibur Rehman under the banner 'Rights of East Pakistan Defence Front', and even engaged Tom Williams to go to Dhaka to assist the defence lawyers. The British press was hostile to Ayub in this case.

On 16 February 1969, an undertrial of the Agartala conspiracy case, Sergent Zahurul Haq, was killed by guards in Dhaka. It was thought to be the mischief ofYahya's intelligence. More than 10 lakh people joined the funeral procession of Haq. There were cases of burning of government houses. Bhasani, a Left-wing leader of East Pakistan, added fuel to the fire by his slogan, 'besiege and burn'. Ayub lamented that 'this man suffers from every kind of disease but does not die' [Altaf]. When the situation in Dhaka worsened, Ayub decided to withdraw the case and release Mujibur Rehman unconditionally.

After the famous crackdown of Bengalis on the night of 25/26 March 1971, Mujib was whisked away to West Pakistan and the case against him was again revived. A sham trial was quickly concluded. The nature of the judgment was not made known. To make Mujib's life miserable, a grave was dug up on one side of Mujib's cell. The mad army junta did not carry out his execution, perhaps due to international pressure. He was cut off from the outside world and knew nothing of Bangladesh war of liberation. Bhutto released Mujib on the understanding that Pakistani POWs in India would be returned forthwith. His political stand was that he would work out a scheme of confederation of the two wings of Pakistan, a bluff to win sympathy from West Pakistanis. The general perception was that the Agartala case was foisted on Mujib when, by evidence, there was nothing against him. This was the army's attempt at eliminating a politician by a judicial process. However, their plotting a false case against Mujib caused the people of East Pakistan to reacted strongly against the army regime.

Such a reaction was not evident during Bhutto's trial and execution. Unlike Bhutto, Mujib was not ditched by his followers in East Pakistan. Gen Musharraf, before the coup, dismissed his own Corps Commander, Tariq Parvaiz, on the ground that he became closer to Nawaz Sharif. After the coup, Mushraff's chosen General, Aziz, started showing his authority by preventing the TV presentation of the budget approved by Gen Musharaff on the ground that the budget prepared by the Finance Minister was not cleared by the GHQ. Gen Musharraf had to stomach this insult. When the chance came, was transferred out to another formation.

7

Poor Functioning of the State-Armed Police Battalions

Sankar Sen

The problem of law enforcement and order maintenance in the country today is compounded by the poor state of health of the State Armed Police Battalions. Armed Police Battalions are the strong arm of the district administration and they come to the aid of district police when the latter finds it difficult to cope with widespread disturbance and continuing lawlessness.

Now, in our country, in each district, there is an armed reserve police kept trained and equipped for intervening in law and order situations. The Indian Police Commission, 1902–03 (Fraser Commission) observed that, 'It is the function of an efficient police not only to prevent and detect crime, but also to secure peace and tranquility of the country.' In addition to the district armed reserve, states have their armed police battalions, more or less organized on the infantry pattern. Among the states that had armed police battalions long before Independence, were Bihar, Bengal, Assam, and Madras. The importance of the district armed reserve and armed police battalions was appreciated even after independence. It was considered not desirable to use the army frequently for dealing with law and order situations, and for containing such situations, the police had to have their own armed units. Addressing the Conference of the State Inspectors General of Police, Sardar Patel said,

> It is even more necessary for State Governments to avoid resorting to military force in the day-to-day administration of law and order. It is from this point of view, and also in full knowledge of the commitments of our army, that I cautioned the provincial Governments in 1947 about the need for self-sufficiency of their police forces. I am glad to say that provincial Governments have generally been very quick in achieving this self-sufficiency and the occasions for calling military in aid of the civil power have been few and far between.

After the Chinese Aggression in 1962, there was rapid increase of armed police battalions all over the country. Their strength has now risen to 426. This overwhelming increase in the number of the armed police in preference to the civil police has often been criticized. It has been argued that armed police battalions have consumed valuable public funds, which could have been better spent for improvement and strengthening of the civil police service to the community. But against the background of mounting danger to internal security emanating from various quarters, increase in the number of armed police battalions was an inescapable necessity.

However, a dispassionate evaluation of the working of the armed police battalions will show that, though they have rendered yeoman service on different occasions and served the country with distinction in inhospitable climes and terrains under daunting conditions, there has been a steady deterioration in the working of these battalions. The standard of discipline, efficiency, and job performance has steadily declined. Immediate steps are called for to reverse this alarming trend.

Poor Leadership

One of the main causes of malfunctioning of the armed police units in the states is the poor quality of leadership. It is a fact that many officers, particularly of the Indian Police Service (IPS), who have not been able to prove their mettle in the district, are dumped into armed police battalions. They dislike it and explore various ways and means of wriggling out of the so-called inconvenient and unglamorous postings. As a consequence, discipline and the morale of the force suffer. For toning up discipline and efficiency of the armed police battalions, the first and foremost need is to improve the quality of officers. The National Police Commission has recommended, in its Sixth Report, while dealing with the IPS, that there should be a central IPS cadre for paramilitary organizations like the Border Security Force (BSF), the Central Reserve Police Force (CRPF) and the Indo-Tibetan Border Police (ITBP). Selected officers from this cadre should be sent to the states as Commandants of the Armed Police Battalions. This will make available to the state governments, a number of police officers with prior experience in commanding armed police battalions in the Government of India. The state governments can gainfully put them in command of the State Armed Police Battalions.

The poor quality of leadership is not confined to the level of Commandants alone. The malaise has spread down the line. I have seen Assistant Commandants of armed police battalions afraid of pulling up the defaulting sepoys and boldly enforcing discipline. In some states, an officer of the rank of Deputy Inspector of Police remains in overall charge of a number of battalions. The National Police

Commission recommends that for effective control and supervision, a Deputy Inspector General (DIG) of Police should be entrusted with five to six battalions (and not 15 to 20, as the Commission had found in some states), so that they would be able to visit the battalions, know first hand, the grievances of the men, and adopt necessary corrective measures. In many states now, there are DGs incharge of armed police battalions and there are Inspectors General (IGs) supervising the work of two or three Deputy Inspectors General of Police (DIGs) of armed police battalions. It is doubtful if this expansion of the hierarchy has improved the functioning of the battalions. Further, IGs and DGs of armed police battalions should be vested with sufficient powers. Very often, they are without financial and disciplinary powers, which put them in an extremely disadvantageous position.

Neglect of Training

Another reason for the poor functioning of the State Armed Police Battalions is neglect of training of the officers and men. This has happened because of gross mismanagement and misuse of trained manpower of the battalions over the years. Very often, armed police battalions are detailed for prolonged law and order duties to the detriment of training. They are deployed in 'ones' and 'twos' on routine police duties like night rounds, controlling crowds before cinema halls, escorting under-trials in the courts, et cetera. As a result, training of men suffers. Its deleterious effect surfaces in critical law and order situations when at times the armed police personnel fail to display proper restraint and go berserk. While posted as DIG Orissa, I was dismayed beyond measure to find armed police units in hilly mining areas are posted for long periods because of continuing labour tension in the area. Men were staying in tents for long spells of time without proper supervision and acquiring the indiscipline of unionized industrial workers. It is absolutely necessary that deployment of armed police personnel should be for a fixed period of time only and the force should be pulled back to the battalion headquarters as early as possible. This, in practice, has become difficult because the District Superintendents of Police (DSPs) invariably try to play safe and requisition more men than are needed and the superior officers feel hesitant to prune the inflated demands.

Curbing excessive deployment of the force is a major challenge for the Central police forces also. Exaggerated demands of the state governments cannot always be resisted by the Central Government as hardly any professional evaluation is undertaken relating to the task to be accomplished. There should also be close scrutiny of the demand and it should always correspond to prior written plans submitted by the states. Immediate deployment without a previously furnished plan should be discouraged.

Poor leadership, prolonged deployment outside without adequate supervision for various odd duties, lack of training, and neglect of genuine grievances are breeding indiscipline in armed police battalions. The truth of the matter is that many of the armed police battalions in different states all over the country are slowly deteriorating with over-use, no training, no rest, and no appreciation of their difficulties. In 1978–79, when police unrest spread like a tidal wave in many states, the armed police units in the states remained in the vanguard of the agitation. Ring leaders of the agitation were mainly from the armed police battalions.

For improving the standard of discipline and efficiency of the armed police battalions, the National Police Commission recommended a Central enactment prescribing uniformity in their composition, officering patterns, and disciplinary rules, et cetera. Armed police units, very often, feel diffident and fail to act as firmly as per law because of the fear of offending the local political bosses. Even a small unit of the army is more effective because it is not limited by such fears. The Central Police forces are also far more effective because they enjoy certain protection under the law and remain accountable to the Central Government only. The courage and confidence of the state police, including the armed police battalions, can be restored only by liberating them from external pressures and influence.

Operational Autonomy

The officers in charge of armed police battalions should be given adequate operational autonomy. Tasks may be prescribed for the units and subunits by the state authorities, but the manpower to be used, the tactics, and logistics should be left to the discretion of the force leaders. Refinement of the training patterns is also of paramount importance. Training of armed police has often remained mired in obsolescence. There is utmost need for upgradation of resources and quality of personnel imparting training. The imperative need to make the training institutions for armed police personnel centres of excellence has unfortunately not been appreciated by the powers-that-be and many of the institutions remain denuded of resources and competent training staff.

It is seen that, during field operations, the armed police battalions gather useful information and valuable intelligence concerning criminal groups, insurgents, and terrorists. But the actionable intelligence gathered during such operations is very often not shared by the concerned authorities. This is an area, where officers supervising the functioning of the armed police battalions and the central paramilitary forces must pay adequate attention. At present, there is only one-way traffic and very few armed police forces are collecting and disseminating useful information.

Attention must also be paid to the human rights sensitization of the armed police personnel. There have been in the past allegations of serious communal bias and caste prejudices displayed by the personnel of the armed police battalions. Officers and men afflicted with caste and communal biases have to be weeded out and there must be constant exhortation to officers and men to inculcate respect for human rights of the citizens, for whose protection they have been deployed.

With the difficult and deteriorating law and order situation in the country there is a constant demand for armed police battalions and the Central police forces. They have to remain well-trained and well-equipped so that the need to call the army in aid of civil authorities is reduced to the minimum. This is a matter of utmost importance. During the first two decades after Independence, serious law and order situations could be tackled by the state police and the Central police forces. Heads of state police forces considered it a matter of professional honour to tackle internal security problems without seeking the army's help. In the 1970s, naxalite agitation at its peak was tackled by the West Bengal Police with the help of CRPF. The army was not called. Later on, overexposure and overdeployment began to tell on the armed police battalions in the state and in the Centre and the army had to be frequently summoned to perform law and order duties. But summoning the army frequently for combatting internal disturbances is bad for the army and also for the country.

8

Internal Security: Perspective and Prescription

Shyamal Datta

It is often said that hindsight helps evolve a foresight by one whose mind is reflective and alert about the surroundings and happenings around. It is this hindsight of events and developments that have gone by, that clearly reveals a phenomenal change in the evolution of security with internal security having become an integral part of national security. Security is no more a mere concern of crime and weapon. It is of a greater concern with respect to safety and dignity of human life. People now expect security to provide freedom from both fear and want.

The growing lumpenization of sections of society, decline in the efficacy of institutions of democracy, and considerable measure of deficit of faith and trust in leaderships at different levels of governance have made the task of ensuring dignity of human life difficult. What annoys the people is the ham-handed enforcement of the rule of law, manifest in the tardy response to frequent assaults on peoples' freedom of movement, liberty, and safety. The rising trend of organized crime, sexual assault, drug trafficking, and acts of violence accentuate the fear, while want is exacerbated by poverty, hunger, corruption, and growing surge of other inequities, injustices, and deprivations of varied kinds.

Fear and want combine to make threats to security diverse, dispersed, and global in character with devastating consequences. Borders become irrelevant and the breach of space, more than the land, has become a defining challenge to sovereignty and territorial integrity. These cataclysmic changes have occurred at a juncture when the State has undergone considerable erosion in its monopoly to use the instrument of force without any deterrence, to enforce order and ensure peace. The weakening in the power and authority of the State has happened over the years, for a variety of reasons. For instance, the monopoly has come under serious challenge, following growing democratization of civil society and non-governmental organizations. These have not only proliferated but have also come to occupy the space that the State has unfortunately been ceding on account of inefficacies of its institutions and inadequacies in the delivery of goods and services.

Civil society groups have come to acquire huge amounts of resources of different types, besides an enormity of reach, networking, and a capacity to challenge and confront the State. They advocate protests, engineer ideas, and galvanize the masses across borders and affiliations in order to cause hurdles to the management of affairs of the State, including development and security in particular. Governance has become far more complex and difficult than before.

What has further debilitated the State is the serious inroads made by the democratization of technology into the State's monopoly with regard to generation of information, overall control on its access, storage, safety, and dissemination. The information highways and super highways that have sprung up in its wake, provide a level playing field enabling one and all, including elements inimical to the interests of the State, to connect with phenomenal speed and ease in order to plan, recruit, train, fund, prepare, and coordinate dastardly plans of action directed against the State, without either crossing the borders or being present at the scenes of crime. Technology also infuses a capacity to spring an element of surprise on the State while perpetrating acts of violence. This, in turn, exposes the chinks in the armour of the State, besides projecting it in a poor light.

The emergence of Internet communication as the most popular channel of connectivity has enhanced the enormity of responsibility of the State and its concerned agencies to keep proper and effective track on the huge volume of traffic on the Internet and its other portals of social networking. In India alone, over 200 million have access to the facility, in addition to over 930 million mobile users as well as millions of subscribers of land, fax, and wireless. On the global plane, over 1.6 billion people are on line and over 4 billion smses are exchanged every day. The mind boggling and ever increasing flow of traffic underscores the most imperative need for an elaborate infrastructure in place to ensure an effective round-the-clock monitoring so as to detect and deter the use of any channel of communication prejudicial to the interests of the State. The vulnerabilities of the State to the growing incidence of cyber attacks, and piracy of information and data to the discomfiture of the State, its leaders, and people are fairly well known in the public domain. And it is not always possible for a developing country to husband adequate resources and spare the same for protection of privacy of people and their safety and security.

What makes the task more herculean is the serious difficulties that the developing countries encounter while keeping pace with the rapid strides in the innovations of new technologies, making the existing ones dated and obsolete. The paucity of resources presents a serious constraint on the path of developing countries to avail of the newer innovations and guard against the dangers often caused by the use of the latest technology by its adversaries. Only the developed countries can afford to do advance planning and mobilize required resources to stay ahead of technological innovations and place adequate effective measures to counter the nefarious designs of inimical elements. Thus, they score a march over acts of hostilities with intervention and interdiction well on time, and before the dangers could materialize. They also spend billions of dollars on regular updating of smart and state-of the art systems to not only thwart the dangers but also to maximize casualties in the enemy camp and optimize the outcome. However, their concern is to secure the systems against hacking, which the adversaries can cause with minimal costs.

The ever expanding dimensions of challenges are so sinister and stupendous that the world's mightiest super powers have not been able to achieve an outright victory in its more than decade long campaign of 'war on terror'. They continue to face an uphill task in containing the scourge of terror, which has since moved from the national agenda to international theatre. *Jihad* has become the defining security challenge of the twenty-first century. It has become an instrument of policy of the *jihadi* groups to try and establish a worldwide theocratic Caliphate, run by the Islamic laws. A sizeable part of South Asia has turned into an epicentre of theocratic nationalism and *jihad*, combined with worst form of religious obscurantism. What has made the *jihadi* threat really dreadful is a genuine apprehension that some of the desperate *jihadi* elements might try to gain access to nuclear devices and weapons of mass destruction and use the same for annihilation of those, whom they perceive to be the 'infidels'. It is said that 9/11 did not turn nuclear not because of a lack of intent but of a lack of capability.

Terror, as an instrument to challenge the establishment, has become popular because of its unnerving impact, comparative lower cost, and publicity mileage. The narratives of discrimination, injustice, humiliation, and alienation are available as ready made fodder to exploit and fuel the anger of not only non-State actors and hostile societies, but also of individuals. They are influenced to embrace the path of terror as a means to carry out senseless killings of innocent people and wanton destruction of public property, which include even economic assets of the people and countries under attack. This has brought the economic security of the State under focus.

Since globalization of the world economy, the dynamics of economic growth and prosperity have undergone a phenomenal change with the removal of trade barriers. This has made the economy huge with international connectivity and networking to stay competitive. The economies of the world have converged on a global platform in a bid to integrate into the global process and maintain their economic presence and relevance. This has led to a mushrooming of economic players and platforms for collaboration and coordination to share knowledge, skills, technology, and market with a view to staying as players of importance. The complexities of new challenges have exposed the State and its vital sectors of R&D to heightened threats of espionage, subversion, theft, physical attack, and accident. The job of guarding economic security has, thus, become far more intricate and challenging than before.

It is rather ironical that the process of economic globalization has, instead of reducing, enlarged the arc of discontent across the world with the youth facing the brunt of its onslaught. This is fairly evident from the 'bloom of myriad springs' in different parts of the world. The springs have been characterized by mobilization of youth from different walks of life, demonstrating frustration and anger of the resurgent middle class and demographic din.The use of information technology comes very handy for a world-wide publicity of anger against the ruling dispensation on socio-economic, ethnic, religious and political issues, affecting the lives of millions. Embedded in these protests is the idea of converting individual action into a collective one against the formidable oligarchies, military dictatorships, and single party dynastic rule. The idea is also to keep the true spirit of democracy alive and connected so that it can spread as a virus of protest pressing for change.

A close scrutiny of such outbursts of mass anger brings to light a well thought-out and calibrated plan of action, whereby a dissent will appear online on the quiet, come into print inoccuously, and grow exponentially before hitting the streets, taking everyone by surprise and bringing to the fore some of the very sensitive and disturbing issues for the groundswell of anger. These protests clearly signal the rise of a new generation of youth who are very alert, sensitive, tech savvy, potent, and powerful to 'stand up against the failure of traditional leaderships and feckless institutions and be counted.' The protests administer a clear warning to politicians and political parties that they should look beyond electoral politics and muster courage to make the hard choice and change.

This 'X or Y' generation is often directly swayed by the 'lure factor' contributed by the countries having improved their economic fortune after the onset of the market economy. The youth get seduced by the glamour of 'economically doing well States' and start believing that they have the right of choice and freedom of movement to respond to the market that beckons and the capital willing to employ them in places other than their places of birth or origin, for achieving a better quality of life. The development has added a new dimension to trans-border migration/immigration with greater mingling of people from across diverse cultures, traditions, and faiths, and made the management of border and coastal security difficult.

No State worth its salt can either insulate or isolate itself from these threats. An inaction will only help the dangers to mature and grow into a deeper malaise and cause existential threat to safety and security. A time will come when the State will find it difficult to defuse the problem and will not be in a position to outsource its responsibility. At the same time, there is no single silver bullet to deal with these complex issues and problems. Therefore, the State has to evolve its own strategy and plans which would call for a multi-thronged, inter-agency, inter-department/ministry and inter-State initiatives for an early evolution of a composite and decisive national security policy with military action not as a solution but as one of the options in the maze of alternatives which come into play according to a broad plan of action, pursued both sequentially and simultaneously, depending on how the situation evolves and unfolds.

It is rather unfortunate that we, in India, continue to remain mired in the past, treating the Police Act of 1861 as our Bible to deal with the problems of the twenty-first century. The governments, both at the Centre and in the states, have shown lack of political will and intent to break from the past and make paradigm shifts in their approach and policies to measure up to the growing challenges of security. As a result, every calamity, man-made or natural, continues to awaken us to the enormity of shortcomings and inadequacies in our security systems. These only help to highlight the challenges and opportunities that we need to confront and avail of respectively. Needless to say, these challenges have moved far beyond the confines of enforcement of law.

Notwithstanding this, we are yet to acknowledge that law enforcement by nature, is reactive, defensive, episodic, and ad-hoc in response. It is so because it is driven by prevention, investigation, detection, and prosecution. It is governed by the rules of evidence to protect the rights of people and uphold the rule of law. It provides the skills and resources that do not promote capacity and capability to take the fight into the enemy camp and effectively neutralize the challenges in a smart way. Its very reactive nature makes the system wait for danger to surface and strike. In sharp contrast to this, today's situation urgently demands in place, an internal security mechanism that is driven by an elaborate network of aggressive intelligence gathering arrangements at different levels with skills, technology and other resources that help detect, deter, and disrupt sources of threat before these could materialize and undermine safety and security. The internal security mechanism is, therefore, known to be proactive, systemic, anticipatory, intutive, innovative, and creative.

There is, however, no denying the fact that Law Enforcement is the main bulwark against crime and violence. In keeping with this, Internal Security and Law

Enforcement have to work in concert and close unison to maximize the outcome of initiatives which will be driven by the philosophy of interdependence, partnership, and multilateralism without, however, giving up the option of unilateral action if the situation so demands. For such a structured response to emerge, there is an urgent need for a change in the mindset of the Indian leaderships at different levels of governance. First of all, the State has to evolve a consensus across the political spectrum, on the need for a doctrinaire approach to security and safety. This can be addressed only after an elaborate and holistic assessment of security environment and challenges with a focus on the State's threshhold of levels of tolerance to varied threats and dangers and its capabilities to deal with these, before firming up what are the paramount interests of the nation and its people irrespective of the political dispensations in office at any point of time. It would involve risk-benefit-cost analysis, examination of options available, choosing of allies and friends, and networking with them, revamping of instituitions and systems, mix of soft and hard power, diplomatic/intelligence offensives, military option, and so on.

While evolving the national security doctrine, the State has to seriously address and take a principled stand across political hues and affiliations on the doctrinaire approach on the application of tools like 'prevention, preemption, interdiction and intervention, hot pursuit, shock and awe, swift, surprise and surgical strikes, responsibility to protect, etc.' Each one of these imperatives would call for building up of adequate capacity and capability of the State to discharge responsibilities for an outcome that would serve its paramount interests. The national security doctrine has to have a counter-terror sub-doctrine with adequate provisions for overt and covert actions with a proactive role to go after the sources of threat and neutralize the same by inflicting deterrent costs. The capabilities will be of such high standards that the State is able to try and stay a few steps ahead of the adversaries, catch them by surprise and sufficiently decapacitate their terror network alongwith, its logistic support and operational bases.

A smart internal security response will need to have a fine tuned interplay of four basic elements of intelligence and warning—prevention and deterrence, crisis and consequence management, and coordinated acquisition and application of technology and equipment. The kinds and degrees of response will be determined on the basis of careful studies and understanding provided by concerned departments, ministeries of the State and Centre, diplomacy, military, security, and intelligence. Idealistically, it would mean that the internal security structure, strategy, and tactics are supplemented by good policies, good politics, and good governance for national safety and security to become strong, stable, and sound. The quality of the application of a national security doctrine on the ground will be measured and judged by the normal flow of life of its people without much fear in mind and want in life. Then only will the State be able to secure safety and security for a dignified life.

9

The Race for Resources and Markets: The Way to Global Domination

Vikram Sood

The State of Play

The next few decades are going to be of great importance to India if it wishes to be a major player on the global theatre. This greatness does not lie in grandiose statements but in the ability to protect its interests and exhibit an internal cohesiveness that gets reflected in international recognition. For this, India will need military power acquired indigenously, substantial rule of law, equitable justice seen to be delivered quickly, economic power, (scientific and technological) and the ability to feed its people, educate them, employ them, and keep them healthy. An estimated 51 million must be given employment by the end of the decade if we want to see substantial progress. A tall order by any standards, but it is necessary to understand the external economic dynamics of this problem in an integrated world. We need to see what is happening around us.

The fabled Silk Route which flourished in the times of the Roman Empire was used to transport spices, gems, and silks from China to Europe has now been revived. Hewlett-Packard despatches 'Made-in-Chongqing' laptops and accessories by train from China to Europe, at least once a week. The Chinese government also announced in July, 2013, that freight trains would run from Zhengzhou in Central China to Hamburg, Germany while DHL, the freight company, would run a weekly express train service from Chengdu to Poland. The quantity shipped may not be as much as by sea, but the routes are shorter and cheaper. Not quite satisfied with this, Kazakhstan authorities are constructing new rail routes that would connect China with Iran through their territory and Turkmenistan, apart from the vast west to east oil and gas pipelines from the Caspian Sea to China.

Separately, the Indian interest in the deep sea port, Chahbahar port of Iran has gathered momentum, and the second phase of the construction could begin soon. This would give India access to Afghanistan, Central Asia and shorten the distance to Europe by 40 per cent and the cost by 30 per cent. The Chahbahar project was partly in response to the Chinese project for the Gwadar Port overlooking the Gulf of Oman and designed for transporting oil from the Gulf and Angola overland into Xinjiang and which has since been completed. The Chinese are learnt to have offered assistance for an airport at Gwadar and to upgrade the Karakoram Highway. This suits Pakistan immensely as it hopes one day to realize its dream as a gateway to Central Asia where the other part of the dream is the TAPI gas pipeline from Turkmenistan through Afghanistan to Pakistan and India.

Meanwhile, the US announced appointment of a special envoy to the cold and virtually uninhabited Arctic. It is no surprise for those watching the next battle for resources and control. The Arctic is the newest battle ground for scarce resources, where the littoral countries, Russia, Norway,

Canada, the USA, and Denmark (Greenland) are prospecting for seabed resources and sea routes for what some say would be the last great resource play. The Chinese are interested, too, as much as the other powers, both as a resource base and a possible shortened sea route for them to the West. The Chinese interest in a pipeline from Kyaukpyu to Yunnan along with a railroad is well documented and the interest in maritime linkages between the Indian Ocean and the Pacific. The latter is now motivated by its growing self-confidence, the need to ensure security of maritime routes, and to pre-empt the US.

Fuelling Growth for Control and Profits

Growing wealth and prosperity globally means stress on natural resources of which oil and gas are the major resources in demand. Continued human prosperity will depend on the quantity and quality of food on the table, forests and fisheries which need continued supply of fresh water, drinking water in the taps, fuel in our vehicles, power stations, precious minerals like coal, copper, and iron, apart from rare earths, for use in manufacture and employment opportunities for the employable to bring the money home for the food. All of these are getting depleted at a rate faster than imagined.

Experts like Michael Klare, in his book *The Race for What's Left*, make the point that even though new resources have been discovered, the world is in an era of tough oil. He refers to the survey report of the International Energy Agency in 2009 which said that 800 oil major fields supplied 68 million barrels a day out of the total production of 80 million barrels. By 2035, this would decline by 75 per cent leaving only 18 million barrels to be produced by these oil fields. A global hunt for the replacement of oil is on.

This will be found in deep underground pockets, or far offshore in inhospitable climates like the Arctic, which is estimated to have oil and gas reserves equivalent to 412 billion barrels of oil and is 56 times the annual US consumption in 2012. Other forms of exploration like the Canadian tar sands, Venezuelan extra-heavy crude, and shale oil are equally expensive and unfriendly. Tracking for shale oil, for instance, involves injections of millions of litres of chemically treated water under high pressure to create fissures in the rock and allow oil to escape. This toxic water cannot be left free and has to be stored or processed. Increased efforts will be made to extract what is called the pre-salt oil, which lies three kilometres under water and then another three kilometres below the salt, sand, rock, and mud dome under the Atlantic Ocean off the coast of Brazil. This makes it one of the most hazardous and expensive endeavours in search for oil.

War zones, inhospitable and inaccessible regions, have also been subject to similar explorations in Iraq, Afghanistan, Iraq, Mongolia, and the Democratic Republic of Congo. Disputed areas have been similarly explored, as in the Falklands by the UK, leading to tensions with Argentina, in the Caspian Sea with its disputed boundaries, and in the volatile maritime zones as in the South China Sea, leading to major power tension between China and the US as well as with other claimants last year.

Mega-corporations have driven and controlled the energy industry. Nations, driven by these corporations, will continue to seek to control this increasingly scarce, difficult and expensive to acquire resource. In the past, too, mega-corporations have used their financial clout and military means in this competition; hostile take-overs and ruthless competition will inevitably continue. Chinese state-owned companies like Sinopec and CNPC will be competing with established Western companies like Shell, BP, and ExxonMobil in Latin America, Africa, and Central Asia. The competition between nations and corporations will be exhausting and vicious. India's mega company, the ONGC, is not yet in the same league. Energy security will remain a top priority for all nations in the twenty-first century as not all of them will have access to nuclear energy. It is not surprising, therefore, that the operational jurisdiction of the US Centcom coincides with the energy producing countries of West and Central Asia meant to provide security to the oil producing nations (except Iran, currently) and to ensure distribution to allied nations.

For some of us, it might escape notice that ExxonMobil represents American power as much as the Pentagon and Centcom do. The company's annual revenues are larger than the economy of a large number of countries, and wherever it operates, it exerts influence over the politics and security of those countries.

The Americans have talked of a grand plan with Afghanistan as the hub, connecting it by road, rail, pipelines, and electricity grids to the Arabian Sea and India, but the Chinese already have their version of the new Silk Road connecting western China to Europe via Central Asia. This would exclude the US from the scheme of things. The Turkmenistan-Afghanistan-Pakistan-India (Tapi) pipeline, driven by American interests to keep Russia, China, and Iran out of the equation, while controlling the distribution of resources, is a non-starter. It is difficult to realistically visualize a pipeline that goes through Afghanistan and Balochistan. The ONGC and China National Petroleum Corp (CNPC) signed an agreement in June for joint exploration in the Sudan, Myanmar, and Syria, something that is viewed with scepticism. This shows just how intricate the world has become. Meanwhile, the southern route from Kunming, Yunnan to Kohima via Mandalay, is something that could be considered by strategic planners.

The strategy evolved in the past by former American Vice-President Dick Cheney stressed on increased domestic production, controlling the oil and gas flow from the Persian Gulf, dominating the sea lanes from the Persian Gulf to the East China Sea, and ensuring Europe reduces its energy dependence on Russia. US President Barack Obama has followed this policy. Libya was more about its oil resources for Europe. The Arab Spring was collateral profit.

Given the need for natural resources and access to oil and gas, areas of the Caspian Sea and the Persian Gulf along with the continental and sea routes through the Indian Ocean up to East China have become extremely vital for continued global economic development. For the foreseeable future, till the discovery and mass usage of alternative sources of energy, the nation which controls these areas, largely controls the world. National strategies, global politics, and power are thus tied with oil as a commodity.

The Elixir of Life

Almost all of 2013, 2014, and in the recent past, the globe has seen unusual weather of excessive heat, snow, rains, and floods. This is easily attributable to climate change but the essence of this in the developing world of Asia and Africa is the dwindling supply of water.

Environmentalists and scientists believe that the biggest potential destabilizers in the world are water scarcity and global warming. Boutros Boutros-Ghali had warned in the 1980s that future wars could be fought over water. His successor, Kofi Annan, was also worried about fierce national competition over water resources that contained the seeds of violent conflict. Ismael Serageldin, Vice-President, World Bank, had predicted in 1995 that 'if wars of this century were fought over oil, the wars of the next century will be fought over water.'

The reason for this worry is not far to seek. Three-quarters of the earth's surface is covered with water but most of it is saline. If the entire water were to be put in a gallon jerry can, then the fresh water available—in rivers, in lakes, and beneath the earth's surface—would just fill a tablespoon. Any loss of this water is permanent and there is no substitute for water. A person can live without food for a month, but only a week without water. Nothing will quench thirst the way water can. Only water can irrigate farms and give life. Unfortunately, mankind has grossly misused and abused this precious life-giver.

By 2025, all of West Asia, Egypt, Libya, Tunisia, Afghanistan, Pakistan, Singapore, and South Africa and parts of India and China will face absolute water scarcity — defined as less than 1,000 cubic metres of water per person per year. These countries would not be able to meet their needs for irrigated agriculture, or for domestic, industrial, and environmental purposes. Water will have to be transferred out of agriculture to other needs, making these countries increasingly dependent on imported food.

If there is no water, then there is no food either. The ecological cycle having been broken, we could get into an endless cycle of droughts, famines, floods and cyclones. The poorer countries will be left with no alternative but to import not only food but also water and oil. The pity is that this could happen to those, who are self-sufficient in food today, and with better water management, even ward off the perils of 2025. But the possibility that the same transnational company could be controlling supply of oil, water, and food only means the return of the East India Company in another incarnation.

Potential conflicts are likely where rivers and lakes are shared by more than one country. The Nile, the Jordan, the Indus, the Ganga, the Brahmaputra, and the Mekong are some of these. In times of water stress and shortages, regions will face water refugees from one region to the other within the country or between two countries.

There could be wars for the control of water supplies; or water resources or systems used as a weapon during a military conflict; or used for a political goal; terrorists could threaten using water sources as a weapon of coercion. Water systems themselves could be targets of military action. Then, with multinational giants having entered the business of supplying water privately, for profit, there could be wars for entrepreneurial control. Inequitable pricing and monopolistic practices have already caused distress in Latin America and South Africa. The most dangerous is naturally the one fought with weapons.

Pakistanis fear that India, as the upper riparian, could one day choke off the Indus waters with disastrous consequences to Pakistani Punjab. Kashmir is thus a matter of life and death. Should the rivers that flow into Pakistan begin to lose their flow because of natural reasons, the Indus Waters Treaty between India and Pakistan will come under stress. Pakistan loses 13 million cusecs of water to the sea every year while sea-water encroaches up to 100 kilometres into Sindh when the Indus water supply declines.

If better water management and all that goes with it are not put in place quickly enough, it is possible that one day reservoirs like the Nagarjuna Sagar or the Nangal or the Mangla Dam could run dry. It is difficult to imagine a situation where the mighty rivers of South Asia become rivulets unable to reach the sea. As the taps run dry and the crops wither away, there would be upheavals—mixed as they would be with regional, caste, sectarian, and communal colour. All this may be difficult to imagine, but this is a calamity waiting to happen. It is a nightmare about to come true.

If there is no change in our pattern of consumption and wastage and pollution, if there is no effort to change our way of life, then that day is not far off when this planet will become a dustbowl. Only sustained early action can prevent this country from becoming a twenty-first century Mohenjo Daro.

Food for Survival

Agriculture is in deep trouble globally. The world's population will increase by about 1.7 billion in the next 20 years—mostly in the Asian and Pacific regions. It will have to be fed but the agricultural innovations of the late twentieth century have peaked. Along with declining productivity, the supply of gas for fertilisers and pesticides, and oil required for machinery and transport is becoming more difficult to obtain and more expensive. Water is fast approaching critical scarcity in the main food-producing regions of the world. Soil fertility is declining because of heavy usage of the soil by industrialized agriculture that tends to neglect rotations and care needed to nurture soil. In fact, the small farmer has been wiped out in countries like USA where the total farming population is less than half the population of New York, and all of it in penury.

Genetically modified (GM) foods and GM seeds, products of modern bio-technology, are touted as the cure for world hunger. This is contested by several activist groups and scientists globally, one of whom had calculated that the money spent on the Iraq war was enough to feed the world's hungry for five years. Governments, anxious to avoid droughts and crop failures and farmer suicides, tend to see the GM revolution as a short-term answer to the problem.

Mankind has over centuries developed its food habits and food. Traditional biotechnology was discovered early when bread was made, or yogurt, wine, or cheese. They were all ultimately a result of manipulating micro-organisms to start the fermenting process—that is how scientists would describe the exquisite Bordeaux or the full Bourgogne. No gene modification is involved.

Modern biotechnology, is however, different and still the subject of debate and even controversy among scientists, environment activists, sociologists, and the big business houses that want to sell the new GM food and seeds. This has involved new techniques as tissue culture, cell culture, and embryo culture. Its application in agriculture has led to GM food claiming to be as good as natural food and GM seeds supposedly having several advantages over traditional seeds. In the USA, where by the end of 1999, two-thirds of all processed food had GM ingredients, no distinction is made between GM food and organic food.

The Europeans have been insisting that GM foods be labelled before the products are put on their supermarket shelves. USA, Canada, and Argentina—the main producers of GM food—see this as an unfair trade barrier and US companies like Monsanto, which have invested massive sums in this technology and totally dominate the GM seed market, have tried to recover their losses by transferring their products elsewhere.

Biotechnology has a lot to offer, but all this is not unmitigated benign technology. Many scientists have doubted this and warned of the dangers that lie ahead and it is not just the fear of the unknown.

In his research paper, 'Biotechnology Briefing—A technology we do not need', David Fleming even argues that GM organisms are not even necessary for agriculture, while Nathan Batalion warns that this is the most potent technology the world has ever known—and more powerful than even atomic energy. Batalion lists 50 harmful effects of GM foods affecting health, environment, farming, as well as its the economic, political, and social threats. Scientists will debate and argue on the effects on health—about the various viruses and bacteria and allergies that could become rampant, and the morality of tinkering with Nature- and it would require many lengthy articles to discuss these fully. The jury on this technique is still out as also on the devastating long-term effects these chemical and powerful weed killers that are sold by megacorporations like Carlyle, Monsanto, Dow Chemicals, and Dupont.

Water-stressed and short-of-arable-land countries like China, South Korea, Saudi Arabia, and India are buying land in Africa as a measure of food security. India seeks to diversify its land holdings through purchases in Tanzania, Kenya, Ethiopia, Malawi, and Mozambique through the MMTC. As the Green Revolution seems to be peaking over, it is imperative that India makes arrangements to feed not only the present population whose food habits have changed and demands have grown, but also the additional 300 million that will be added to the population by 2050. Private corporations and banks in the West have begun investing in agricultural land as the new profit-making venture. Aginvesting is the new pursuit.

Conflict Copper and More

In September 2010, the Japanese arrested a Chinese fishing

captain, who had been accused of ramming his trawler into Japanese coast guard vessels in the East China Sea. As the tension escalated, international media announced on 22 September that Chinese customs officials were stopping all shipments of rare earths used in high technology production from mobile phones to hybrid cars to Japan. The Chinese were retaliating without saying so. The contentious issue was the long-running dispute over the ownership of the Senkaku/Diaoyu Islands and reaction was economic pressure over the incident.

Rare earths used in a variety of applications in the manufacture of modern equipments of military (from tail fins of the F-22 Raptor aircraft to lightweight batteries in commercial use) are the latest arenas for possession and control. The disturbing aspect is that China has completely monopolized the mining, processing and refining of these rare earths up to even 97 per cent according to some estimates. The hunt for these rare earths elsewhere continues amidst seeking to control other minerals mostly copper, iron, bauxite, coal, and other critical material like uranium, lithium, manganese, titanium, platinum, to name a few. The contest for ore reserves of iron and copper will be fought in Afghanistan, Guinea, and the Arctic. For India, the only real choice is Afghanistan followed by Guinea. Almost all of the West African States are endowed with mineral resources with conflict-ridden countries like Guinea providing one-tenth of the world's bauxite supply apart from huge reserves of iron ore.

In our neighbourhood, both Myanmar and Afghanistan have been of interest to China. The Chinese Metallurgical Group Corporation was awarded a 30-year-old, $3-billion contract in the Anyak copper mines in 2007. The Steel Authority of India Limited (SAIL) has won a $10 billion bid for investment in iron ore and Pakistan Petroleum and India's Oil and Natural Gas Corporation (ONGC) are now bidding for six exploratory blocks varying from 1,220 to 2,200 square miles north of Mazar-e-Sharif. There are other contenders also but it is suspected that the Chinese have withdrawn in favour of the Pakistani bid. The blocks are estimated to contain a billion barrels of oil. Besides, India is also the largest donor of aid to Afghanistan ahead of Japan and the US.

Afghanistan has become an investment-cum-exploration destination only recently, but the Chinese have been active there for nearly a decade. Despite the efforts made in the last 17 years, Steve Levine, author of *The Oil and the Glory,* writes that the West has been unable to access the oil and gas fields of Kazakhstan and Turkmenistan. On the other hand, the Chinese were able to get a deal for an on-shore natural gas field in Turkmenistan in 2006 and build a 1,700 kilometre pipeline into China by 2009.

China has taken advantage of the earlier US retreat or disinterest in Africa, following its preoccupation in Iraq and Afghanistan, and has moved in there in strength. It has long-term interests in the Indian Ocean Region. Eventually, China will build a strong enough navy to be present in the region.

The ultimate winner in this quest for resources and markets for the purpose of global domination will not be that nation which acquires control of these reserves. In addition, it will be that country that adapts best to preservation, innovation, and substitution. Technologies that save not destroy or create non-degradable waste that will be the cause for collapse. Wars could be fought for resources and markets, for profit and wealth; twenty-first century colonialism may not be much different from the earlier one except in scale and style, and for that, well-armed and equipped armed forces will remain.

10

Security Challenges in Manipur and Tripura in North East

B.L. Vohra

The Northeast has always been a security challenge for India since Independence, starting with Nagaland initially and continuing to the entire region even today after 68 years. The latest challenge is the racial attacks on the youth of that region in Delhi in the beginning of 2014; though this challenge is of a different kind. Of the eight sisters (Sikkim has been added later), the situation is generally call, except in Assam and Manipur. Assam has been having problems of ULFA, Bangladeshi illegal migrants, demands of Bodoland et cetera. Manipur, an erstwhile princely state is the worst hit because it is a small area with much less population than Assam and yet the violence there has been going on unabated for decades except in the recent past. In sharp contrast, is Tripura, another erstwhile princely state with a small population, where the state government, through strong political will backed by the local police, has tackled insurgency and the state is peacefully on the road to development.

The people of Manipur have been facing violence for many decades now. Sometime back, we read about bomb blasts close to the residence of the Chief Minister in Imphal, the state capital, and it was not for the first time. We can only imagine the situation in the rest of the state. The people of Manipur are suffering both at the hands of more than two dozen insurgent groups of Meities, Nagas, and Kukis on the one hand and the security forces on the other hand. Ambushes, murders, kidnappings, extortions, et cetera, have been going on for a long time, though of late, the violence is rather low. There is no economic development. In fact, there is only suffering. In the interiors, there is not enough drinking water, electricity, roads, schools, dispensaries, et cetera, and the poverty continues. Then there is economic blockade by the Nagas for long periods on the main highway from Dimapur to Imphal leading to more economic sufferings. There is no political will to tackle the situation in Manipur and this, in turn, is due to deep-rooted corruption in the state led by the politicians and followed by police, bureaucracy, and others, of course with honourable exceptions. The Central Government is a milch cow and most of the money being sent by it is being pocketed in one form or the other.

A landlocked state with a valley in the middle and hills around it, Manipur is primarily inhabited by the Meities, mainly the Hindus, and Kukis in the valley and Nagas and Kukis in the hills. All three communities have their aspirations and all took to guns to fulfill these aspirations. Whereas the Naga insurgency is quite old, the main group now fighting for independence is NSCN (I-M). Both Issac and Muviah, after whom the faction is named, belong to the Ukhrul district of Manipur. Currently, as of there is a ceasefire of the Central Government with this group and negotiations have been going on for a long time on its demand of autonomy within the Indian Constitution (earlier they were demanding a separate country).

They have also been wanting a merger of the Naga-inhabited areas of Manipur with Greater Nagaland, which is not acceptable to Manipur. Then, the Meities in the valley have also been demanding independence and have many underground groups starting with United National Liberation Front (UNLF), Peoples' Liberation Army (PLA), PREPAK, KCP and many others. These days Manipur Peoples' Army (MPA) consisting both of UNLF and PLA is strongest. These groups have been a force to reckon with by indulging in lot of violence like NSCN. The Kukis are following the same path and have groups demanding a separate homeland though there is a ceasefire with a few groups these days. But essentially, most of these two dozen groups are extortionists and criminals. Since there are no economic opportunities in the state, this has created a serious security situation. With the international border with Myanmar, many of these groups have their camps on the other side and we have not been getting any help from that country due to its own problems. Then, China has been fishing in troubled waters by giving training and weapons earlier and may now also be continuing to do so.

The police are under tremendous pressure all the time. Even though the Central Reserve Police Force (CRPF), Assam Rifles, and the army are there for decades now, no real difference in the situation is there. People have been demanding withdrawal of Armed Forces Special Powers Act (AFSPA). We have all heard of the iron lady, Irom Sharmila in Manipur, who is on fast for more than a decade on this issue. It is a pity that such a wonderful state in the lap of nature, with lovely people, which is also called the sports factory of India in the form of well-known players in all disciplines playing all over the country for different teams (remember Mary Kom, the recent Olympic Bronze Winner boxer, who incidentally now is the Superintendant of Police (SP) in Manipur Police) is having this fate with no light anywhere on the horizon.

Tripura also had its brand of violent insurgency from the 1970s onwards. It was a state of tribals. After the partition of India, Hindus from Bangladesh came in large numbers to Tripura and became the majority population in the state. They captured the land of the tribals, trade, commerce, and politics and became the rulers. The tribals, having been driven away, took up arms, demanding their own homeland and wanting the migrants to be driven away. The insurgency there was fuelled earlier by Pakistan, from East Pakistan, and later by Bangladesh through their intelligence agencies. Islamic fundamentalism in Bangladesh added to the problems. Even though Tripura played an important role in the liberation of Bangladesh, its long border with that country (it is surrounded by Bangladesh from three sides) has been more of a problem with most of the insurgents of Tripura and even others of the Northeast establishing camps there, aided and abetted by that government. Violence, kidnappings, ambushes, murders, and arson were the order of the day from the mid-1970s up to the year 2000, when the state took on the insurgents. The state police, backed by strong political will took on the main insurgent groups of National Liberation Front of Tripura (NLFT), All Tripura/Tribal Front of Tripura (ATTF) and others with no help from the Army but backed mainly by CRPF. Today, there is peace in the state. Of course, there are the usual kinds of crime there now, with an increase in rape, et cetera, but insurgency has withered away, though there is need of keeping a close watch. The state government there is giving its due to the entire population spread all over the state by running an honest and efficient administration with a tight control on money. The main reason for this success has been the political will of the honest Chief Minister Manik Sarkar of the CPM. And this trait of honesty follows in the police, bureaucracy, and elsewhere generally. Because of this, Sarkar last year won his fourth term as Chief Minister. Personally, he is known to be the poorest Chief Minister in the country with only about Rupees Ten Thousand with him and no car, house, or any other property and bank account. The people there are so happy with him that they elected CPM again against all odds, even when it was washed away in West Bengal and Kerala, where it had been ruling for a long time.

Reverting to Manipur, since the state government has failed to show any results mainly due to lack of political will, logically, the Central Government should have stepped in effectively. But Manipur is far too away from Delhi to merit any attention. Moreover, it has just two MPs, which count for nothing in a house of 543 members. So, politics is responsible for the mess there. The institution of having an elected state government, which is applicable across the board in India and is based on the Constitution, has not paid dividends here.

Twice during informal meetings, I asked Shri P. Chidambaram, when he was the Union Home Minister, as to why Manipur couldn't be sorted out. He told me, 'The Chief Minister. There is a problem.' So they know here at the Centre also that the politicians are the main reason behind this situation there, but can't do or don't want to do anything about it. I also told this twice to the Prime Minister, again during informal meetings. He knew the problem and asked me to suggest a solution. I told him to have President's Rule for a long duration. Obviously, that is not possible due to the democratic system adopted by us across the board in the country. The tragedy is that everybody knows what is wrong there and yet nobody is doing anything about it, or shall we say, is unable to do anything because of the democratic system that we have adopted. It is good to have elections, have representatives in the state assemblies, and the majority party ruling the state. But if the states quo is no longer working in any particular state of the country, should we not have a provision for a different set up in case of such a need?

One way could be to have President's Rule with the best of bureaucrats, serving or retired, from all over the country to work in the state in all areas of work. They should be given double the pay of the last pay drawn and surely the matters will improve. But according to the present constitutional provisions, President's Rule can be imposed in a state in certain circumstances, of which the current ones as in Manipur are not included. Moreover, President's Rule is only for a short period—generally for six months and sometimes up to one year. This period is not long enough for improvement in states like Manipur. And we can't send honest, efficient politicians from other states (though hardly any are available) on deputation to places like Manipur!

In my humble view, there should be a constitutional amendment giving much more powers to the Governor to rule the state with an advisory council of the local people's representatives, elected or otherwise. And this should be for a minimum period of five years to begin with. Perhaps during that time, the public will be able to throw up good, honest and efficient politicians, who can take up the reins of the state government. Meanwhile, the Central Government has to make sincere efforts on all fronts, including being diplomatic with the bordering countries for a just and peaceful Northeast along with the rest of India.

Let me also add that I am not holding any brief for the CPM, neither saying that it is a good party nor stating that the Congress is a bad party. It is the leadership in the states that matters. In Punjab, it was the Congress Chief Minister Shri Beant Singh, who showed the political will to tackle insurgency and even laid down his life. In Tripura, it is the CPM that has succeeded.

A word about the functioning of the police would be in order here. It is the same police all over India. It is competent and can deliver, provided it is given the political backing and resources. Punjab, Tripura, and Andhra Pradesh have been outstanding examples. How is it that the same policemen can deliver results in Tripura and not in Manipur? Of course, the police leadership has also to rise to the occasion.

11

Private Security Agencies in India

D.C. Nath

The growth of private security agencies in India has not been a fairy tale. They emerged as a natural process out of sheer necessity but gained roots based on hard toil under adverse conditions. Increasing accumulation of large properties by individuals and growing industrialization in a developing economy provided soft targets to criminals and rivals alike. Their protection by the state authority was no longer feasible. People, therefore, started gathering their own strength and more enterprising ones formed their own security systems or obtained that from a newly-formed profession, known as 'private security agencies'.

In these circumstances, professionalism in private security was a far cry. B.N. Mullik, the legendary police officer, who was the Director of the Intelligence Bureau of the Government of India, was the first Indian to visualize the importance of national security duty being performed by these agencies. In the early 1960s, he set up a wing of Industrial Security in the Intelligence Bureau. Apart from sending out Central Industrial Security Inspection teams to audit the performance of these agencies and the extent of security being provided to the industry owners (both government and private), this wing simultaneously started training programmes on industrial security. Thus, the seeds of professionalism in private security were sown and the subject of Industrial Security started developing as a discipline in the field of overall national security interests.

The burgeoning growth of private security agencies all over the country soon attracted the attention of the law-enforcing authority. The need for regulating their growth was discussed in a conference of the Inspectors General of Police in the late 1980s, and finally, a Private Security Agencies (Regulation) Bill was tabled on the floor of Parliament in 1994. Some apparent pitfalls in the Bill having been brought to notice. The Minister of Internal Security had then asked the International Institute of Security and Safety Management (IISSM), an apex body of security service providers, users, and consultants, to suggest improvement. An expert committee headed by a former Director of Central Bureau of Investigation (CBI) was formed. The committee's recommendations lay buried in the ministry for years. Finally, with the IISSM pursuing the matter in association with the Bureau of Police Research and Development (BPR&D), the Ministry of Home Affairs, Government of India, a revised Bill was prepared. Eventually, the Bill got through, and on 22 June 2005, the Private Security Agencies (Regulation) Act (PSAR Act) was enacted.

The PSAR Act is a milestone in the history of the growth chart of private security agencies in the country. Even though the Act did not satisfy the requirements for smooth progress of private security, the Act, for the first time officially, recognized the important role of private security agencies as a profession. The salient features of the Act are:

- Every private security agency has to be licensed company-wise, that is, individual security guard or supervisor cannot get a licence, as in vogue in the US.

- Each employee of such licensed companies will have to have a certificate of training. Thus, security training has been compulsory, leading the way to bring about the much-needed professionalism among the security practitioners in the country. The Act lays down specific course details also.
- The companies will also have the character and antecedents of all their employees duly verified from the police, according to a prescribed format.
- The licensing authority is the Joint Secretary in the Home Department of the state governments.
- Licensing will be district-wise and state-wise, depending on the operational jurisdiction of these agencies. There is no system of an all-India licence as in the case of, say, a driving licence or a gun licence. This is a big lacuna in the Act functionally.
- All private security companies working in the country will have to be registered in India after due verification of their antecedents and will be denied a licence if they have a proprietor or a majority-shareholder, partner or director, who is not an Indian.
- Conditions for cancellation of licences laid down in the Act include, inter alia, compliance with some statutory regulations covering payment of minimum wages, provident fund, gratuity, bonus, et cetera.

There is, however, a big 'catch' in the entire situation. The PSAR Act 2005 is a Central Act and Central Model Rules under this Act have also been prepared. This Act has to be passed by State Legislatures for implementing the provisions of the Act/Central Model Rules. Only a handful of States/Union Territories have so far adopted this Act. And even where the Act/Model Rules have been adopted, there has hardly been much of enforcement. Thus, the Act and the Central Model Rules brought out for regulating the functioning of private security agencies and making them truly professional, have virtually remained on paper. There is apparent reluctance on the part of the private security agencies to be regulated, but the Central Government, who quite rightly enacted this Act, does not also seem to be keen on successful implementation of the provisions of the PSAR Act, 2005. Even with many defects, the Act has great potential to streamline the functioning of private security agencies from running only as money-earning organizations, as they seem to be in reality. The virtual bureaucratic indifference to enforce the Act reflects their lack of understanding of the great complementary role the private security agencies can play to help government agencies sub-serve national security interests.

Private security agencies can be of various types. Some of these provide only man-guarding service, both armed and unarmed. Others provide only technological aids to security, whereas some are engaged primarily in detective services only. There are, however, some agencies combining all these services. Yet another specialist service emerging relates to providing executive protection services alone, that is, personal security to commercially important persons (CIPs), members of their families, or such other 'very important person' (VIPs) in the private sector.

Then, there are two distinct systems of maintaining security system: one is the proprietary type, that is, the managements' own team, and the other is contractual, that is, one hires the services of private security agencies on a contract basis. Large, Public Sector Units (PSUs), Multinational Corporation (MNCs) or private sector industries, however, have both types, that is, a combination of both proprietary and contractual systems of security.

The legal basis of private security agencies working in the field is provided by the sections concering the rights of the private defense of body or property as provided in the Indian Penal Code (Sec 96 to Sec 106). Basically, being the outcome of individual enterprise, all private security agencies started with personal contacts and hiring of retired policemen or armed forces personnel. Now, the large players in the field take direct graduate trainees, who are put through some basic training courses and thus take security as their chosen career. Some of these graduate trainees are highly competent and turn out to be true professionals in the field of private security. Of late, MBA students or executives with MBA qualification have also started joining private security agencies, thus pushing out, in many cases, the retired folk from the armed forces or the police services. However, a large contingent of retired armed force officers find place in the supervisory rank—thanks to the government's policy of resettling them through the Directorate General of Resettlement.

A significant advance made by the industry relates to the application of science and technology to security service. Indigenous security-related equipment manufacturers with dedicated research wings have emerged. Some of them are proving their worth in providing systems integration on customized basis in the highly competitive market dominated mostly by established MNCs from abroad. It is, therefore, good to see some tech-savvy security professionals in a number of big establishments. Side by side, competent security executives are also learning the tricks of IT security, an exclusive and specialized field until recently. Consequently, enlightened business houses are facilitating convergence of all streams of security services, namely, man-guarding systems, electronic security systems and IT security management. However, there remains a vast scope for fuller development in this direction.

How big the field of operation of these private security agencies is, is a moot question. Some authentic information was first provided by BIRD, a specialist unit of IMRB International, in 2005. According to that survey, there were 15000 private security agencies in India and the overall manned security market size was estimated at Rs. 50 billion or more. In the first decade of the twenty-first century, the industry was expected to grow at a rate of 20–25 per cent annually. According to an estimate done by the Central Association of Private Security (CAPSI), an industry trade group, in 2009, this industry employed 5.5 million people through about 5500 security companies. For all practical purposes, it was a guess-estimate and the actual figures today (2013) would be much more. It is now estimated to be a Rs. 22,000 crore business and it is reportedly growing at 15–20 per cent annually. ASSOCHAM expects it to cross Rs. 40,000 crore by 2015. The security industry's growth rate is 25 per cent over the past 5-7 years and by the end of 2013, it is anticipated to grow much faster. India is expected to become one of the major civil security markets in the world with expected cumulative spent of about US$ 10 billion by 2017. That's a more conservative estimate than the one by Frost & Sullivan, which expects security spending—including homeland security and equipment bought by government agencies— to cross Rs 54,000 crore by 2016. That sounds plausible, considering the global private security industry is pegged at US $200 billion, and growing at 14 per cent every year. The US market accounts for 42 per cent of that, followed by Western Europe at 26 per cent and Asia Pacific at 12-13 per cent. By 2015, India will have at least 4 per cent share, making it among the top 10 markets for security.

The bulk of the private security industry (about 93 per cent) comprises services, such as, manned guarding, electronic security-related services, for example, alarm monitoring, CCTVs, fire alarms systems, and cash-in-transit services. The balance is accounted by equipment manufacturers, such as, Honeywell, Bosch, and Siemens and specialized services, such as, detective investigation, employee verification and personal security. Some of these agencies have also started spreading their operations outside India, acquiring established security agencies in countries like the UK and Australia in recent times. If one could compare with the growth rate of the private security industry in the USA, where the manpower strength of private security agencies outstrip that of the government's law-enforcing agencies by as high as 3:1, the private security agencies in India are also likely to register such exponential growth in the emerging sensitive security ambience in the country.

These agencies are also diversifying or expanding their areas of activities, approximating the concept of truly functioning as an auxiliary police force in the country. Some of them provide services like, escort of high value individuals or cash, vault/ATM security, security in exhibitions, and security to heritage monuments, hospitals, academic institutions, museums, hotels, and banks. The services of private security agencies have been put to use not only in large-scale police *bandobast*s during religious festivals or general elections, but also occasionally in 'guarding' police stations, thus allowing policemen to perform routine police functions like crime control. There are indications that some degree of specialization in providing security services in specific areas is also taking roots, thus showing growth of professionalism in the industry.

An area where the leaders of the industry will have to pay adequate attention is security training, which, in India, is nowhere near the required level in terms of content, competence, or even infrastructure. Barring a very few agencies, the vast majority neither has a proper training system nor are they inclined towards spending money on training, a typical failure noticed in almost all fields. A number of professional bodies, of both national and international calibre, are working in the field with the ostensible objective of promoting or raising the level of professionalism in the industry, but their activities mostly remain mired in professional rivalry or one-upmanship.

However, in spite of all limitations, private security agencies are playing a significant role in protecting the overall national economy and in sub-serving national security as well. Their services can be harnessed into national security duties such as in counterterrorism strategy only if the state authority would make efforts to take steps in encouraging them and getting them duly involved, as is being very successfully done in many countries in the West, with the London Police showing the way. The agencies have shown willingness to join hands with the government, but the government still does not repose enough trust in them nor does it show much interest in encouraging them to develop professionally. If the state authorities show interest in enforcing the provisions of the PSAR Act alone, to start with, national security interests would be better served by these agencies.

12

Are We Effective in Countering Terrorism?

D.C. Pathak

The new alerts from the Intelligence Bureau about further attacks by the Indian Mujahideen and Lashkar-e-Toiba and the continuing threat of Naxalism draw attention to the fact that, for nearly two decades now the handling of these prime challenges to national security have not yielded lasting results, probably because we are still tentative not only about their origins but also about the policy response needed to deal with them. 'Advent of the new regime led by Prime Minister Narendra Modi is making a welcome difference.' Consequently in the fourth line substitute 'had' for 'have' and in the fifth line of the para substitute 'were' for 'are still'.

It was in the mid-1990s that Indian intelligence unearthed the covert plans behind cross-border terrorism and Naxalism that were to unfold in subsequent years, exactly as predicted. In the first case, it was clearly reported how the Pakistani Inter Services Intelligence (ISI) credited for the success of the anti-Soviet armed campaign in Afghanistan, had decided to replicate the Afghan Jihad in Jammu & Kashmir by infiltrating Mujahideen across the

LoC and to enlarge that offensive into a proxy war by sending in trained militants across the porous Indo-Nepal and Indo-Bangladesh borders to carry out terrorist attacks on targets in other parts of India as well. The adversary succeeded in inflicting losses on India ranging from the 1993 serial blasts at Mumbai to the 2013 twin blasts at Hyderabad 2013 with an unprecedented 26/11 carried out in between.

As regards Naxalism, it was again in the mid-1990s that the Intelligence Bureau unravelled the plan of the underground Naxalite leadership to operationally unite the Maoist Communist Centre (MCC) of Bihar and the People's War Group (PWG) of Andhra Pradesh by utilizing the intervening Dandakaranya forest belt as the corridor. The ambitious plan even envisaged spread of the movement to the Northeast where it would seek linkage with the left- of the centre insurgent groups active in the region. In spite of the initial success of the Andhra Pradesh Police in combatting the movement militarily, Naxalism steadily spread across the map of India and became a trans-national threat. Today, it is posing a serious challenge to our para military forces in the forest and hilly terrains of Chhattisgarh, Maharashtra, and Odisha and beginning to form units in urban centres as well.

Cross-border terrorism and Naxalism have different origins, support base, and methodology of execution of their violent operations. In the first case, the enemy is external and is set upon causing political and economic destabilization of India by covertly pumping in terrorists, funds, and other forms of support to keep up the offensive. The adversary has developed not only the capacity to organize an attack from outside as in 26/11, but also the capability of carrying out acts of terrorism through its trained underground modules locally raised within the country. A deceptive period of quiet only indicates further planning as the current intelligence alerts show.

Naxalism, originating in West Bengal in the late 1960s went through an uncertain period of advocacy of the Maoist doctrine of 'power coming through the barrel of the gun' before it gained ascendancy in the 1990s and rapidly spread to new areas on the strength of its underground organizational planning, rising number of trained cadres, and acquisition of arms and explosives. The enlargement of Naxalism, now better described as the Maoist movement, occurred because of the combination of an ideological pull, the atmospherics of disgruntlement prevailing in the remote interiors of India, particularly, in the tribal belts, and the unfortunate 'withdrawal' of local administration in the affected areas on the first appearance of gunmen, thus making it easy for the Maoists to build a 'parallel government'.

What has come in the way of a sustainable strategy being developed against these prime threats is the unwillingness of the political leadership to accept that while the police and Law&Order are in the domain of the state, dealing with issues of national security requires a 'joint-ness' of Centre and the states. In a situation, where the agencies garnering intelligence relevant to national security are spread across various wings of the government, there is still no effective arrangement at the national apex to get the total information on a major threat to converge at a common point. The NCTC ran into a problem because it blurred the line between the covert turf of information handling and the legal domain of arrest, search, and seizure that belonged to the state police in our system.

In a democratic dispensation, it is extremely important that national security concerns do not get meshed into domestic politics in any manner. In the joint handling of these threats, the Centre should be the lead player on terrorism and the states should be in the lead as far as Naxalism is concerned. The response to both cross-border terrorism and the Maoist militancy has to be professional, in the sense that no individual is touched on mere suspicion but held only on evidence.

In dealing with cross-border terrorism, 'peace talk' diplomacy should not become an end in itself. On Naxalism, our polity should allow a line to be drawn between those, who merely support the leftist ideology without upholding violence and the gun-wielding Naxalites, who are often neutralized by the forces of the State with minimal collateral damage. The strategy has to be to restore normalcy in identified districts and then join up the islands of peace so that these are held together for development.

The issues related to the handling of terrorism require a scrutiny of the functioning of our intelligence set up and an in-depth examination of the strategic scene that provides the backdrop to the threats facing India. An interesting development of the post-Cold War era was the emergence of two new versions of war—the 'proxy war' and its counter, the 'pre-emptive' war. It is ironic that Afghanistan, living up to its reputation as 'the geographical pivot of history', first caused the demise of one superpower in the beginning of the nineties and then became the territory from where a new kind of offensive, by way of global terror, would be launched against the sole superpower left at the end of the Cold War. A proxy war was a covert offensive that used cross border terror as its instrument. The atrocity of 9/11 became an expression of its most destructive form and potential. In the course of the retaliatory 'war on terror' that followed under the aegis of the US-led coalition, the war on

Iraq emerged as the first example of a pre-emptive war of the new post-Cold War era.

Considering the fact that intelligence plays a crucial role in deciding the issues of war and peace, it is interesting to find that in these first illustrations of proxy war and pre-emptive war, the question of intelligence became the lead story. While 9/11 exemplified the classic intelligence failure in the sense that advance information was missing, the war on Iraq—as it turned out—was a case of falsehood catered as intelligence. When the American Chief Inspector of weapons, David Kelley, said he found 'evidence of intent' in Iraq, he fell short of discovering any plan of Saddam's regime against the US. The pre-emptive war was questioned because of both flawed 'information' and a tinted 'analysis'. That Saddam Hussain ran a despicable dictatorship and had to go became the only plea of defense for an otherwise unjust attack.

For India, this matter is of particular significance as the country has been facing a vicious proxy war from a hostile neighbour, who uses cross-border terrorism as its instrument in pursuance of a design to replicate Afghan Jihad in Kashmir and picks up targets in the rest of India as well, for terrorist attacks. Even though India had come on board with the US-led Coalition against Global Terror before Pakistan joined it, Pakistan pursued its covert cross-border offensive against India, without any fear of disapproval from the Western camp. 26/11 was India's 9/11 but it saw the US not upholding India's stand that the Pakistani army and ISI were complicit in that horrendous attack. The increasing American dependence on Pakistan in conducting the 'war on terror' against Islamic radicals explained this unhelpful attitude of a friendly superpower, but it also reaffirmed the reality that, notwithstanding the arrangements of 'sharing of intelligence' with friendly countries, India had to have the best possible intelligence set up in place.

The matter of adequacy of our intelligence to measure up to the complicated task of countering the proxy war assumed a new found importance and invited professional scrutiny after 26/11. Since Pakistan had used India-specific outfits under its control like Hizbul Mujahideen and Lashkar-e-Toiba—which are different from the Taliban-Al Qaeda combine—as instruments of cross-border terrorism against this country, it was solely the Indian responsibility and concern to launch suitable countermeasures for pre-empting their mischief. The challenge for our intelligence agencies has now become truly formidable with the increasing spread of the ISI-linked Indian Mujahideen modules of locally raised elements in several states. Indian intelligence agencies have performed well and neutralized a number of underground modules of terrorists created by the adversary on our soil.

Most major countries have a plurality of intelligence agencies and this does raise the issue of coordination. Further, information of intelligence value comes not only from the intelligence organizations, but also from other channels such as the watchful observations of the country's Missions abroad and the regulatory agencies overseeing the borders and the international financial transactions. Even the material accessed on the information super highway and vetted by analysts, is found useful for preparing security estimates. Complete intelligence is difficult to come by and this is why it is important that strategic intelligence from various sources flows to a common apex where the comprehensive picture of the threat would be drawn up. It may be recalled that the Subrahmanyam Committee Report on Kargil had listed out over sixty intelligence inputs furnished by the civil and military agencies through the second half of 1998, which never reached the assessors at the top.

Amongst the agencies there has to be a mandated sharing of relevant information. Most countries have separate organizations responsible for internal and external intelligence. In India the RAW was carved out of Intelligence Bureau (IB) in 1968. As the new agency expanded, it had to face the natural challenge of getting its sourcing right and grooming its new recruits in the complex discipline of intelligence. This is an ongoing task for an intelligence organization anyway. Intelligence is a highly professional discipline resting on distinct precepts and principles. It is rooted in logic of thought, awareness of human behavior, and an ingrained ability to distinguish essentials from non-essentials. In a situation where the most serious of domestic threats—terrorism and proxy-war—originate from outside our frontiers, it is important that organizational independence notwithstanding, there should be functional unity between these two agencies. This has been achieved substantially but has to be institutionalized further. The appointment by the Modi government of a National Security Advisor (NSA) with intelligence background has been a step in the right direction.

Overseeing the work of coordination among the intelligence agencies can be done by professionals, who have had a life-long experience of this discipline and who are known for their dedication to the national interests. There is merit in the view that this function could be performed in a participative mode by an Intelligence Board headed either by NSA himself or by a National Intelligence Advisor working in tandem with the former and including the Chiefs of the Intelligence agencies as well as the head of the Joint Intelligence Committee (JIC). The first maxim of intelligence is that national security does not admit of a divided turf. The Intelligence Board should upgrade the systems of coordination, exchange of information between the Centre and the state intelligence organizations, and reporting to the government. The National Intelligence Advisor should handle the functions of accountability to the parliamentary forums and take responsibility of internal oversight of the agencies by looking into any case of professional misconduct within the agency for advising the political executive on the follow up. None of this must come in the way of complete operational independence of the individual agency. The threats of terrorism and Naxalism can become more intense as the situation in Afghanistan turns favorable for Pakistan, on the one hand, and the possibility of Maoist insurgency acquiring an external input from our adversaries increases, on the other.

13

Menace of Bangladeshi Infiltration and its Impact on National Security

Ram Kumar Ohri

In the recent past the tectonic after-effects of the illegal infiltration from Bangladesh were witnessed across West Bengal. On October 2, 2014, around 12:00 noon an explosion occurred in a two-storeyed building in the Khagragarh locality of Burdwan. The building was owned by one Nurul Hasan Chowdhury, who used to stay in another house across the road. Hasan Chowdhury was a leader of the Trinamool Congress and the ground floor of the building was used as Trinamool Congress party office. During the 2008 and 2013 Panchayat elections, the house was used as the election office by the Trinamool Congress. When the police arrived on the scene after being informed by local residents about an explosion and smoke billowing out of the first floor room, they were prevented from entering the house by two women inmates at gunpoint. They were the wives of terrorists Shakil Ahmed and Abdul Hakim and threatened to blow up the building in case the police dared to enter. Before the police could enter the building the two women had allegedly destroyed several documents which could be used by police as evidence of terrorist activities.

Shakil Ahmed, who had rented the place from Hasan Chowdhury hailed from Karimpur in Nadia district. Due to the bomb blast he died on the spot, while two other terrorists were injured. One of them Sobhan Mondal died later at the Burdwan Hospital. The other terrorist named Abdul Hakim, from Lalgola in Murshidabad district, was admitted to the hospital in a critical condition. The wives of Shakil Ahmed and Abdul Hakim and their two children were left unharmed by the chance bomb blast. The police arrested the two women and recovered nearly 55 improvised explosive devices, wrist watch dials and RDX from the house. The police also recovered several SIM cards and tools used for making improvised explosive devices along with Micro SD cards containing Islamic propaganda songs and Taliban training videos. Several fake ID documents like electoral cards, passports, maps and half burnt books in Arabic were also recovered.

Preliminary investigations by the West Bengal CID indicated that a militant group called, *'al Jihad'* was involved in manufacturing bombs. According to informed sources, the *al Jihad* module had planned a series of ten blasts in Kolkata during the Durga Puja. To their dismay, soon they found that the terror network of Jamat-ul-Mujahideen Bangladesh was not limited to the State of West Bengal. The outfit's jihadi activities had struck deep roots in several other parts of India, including Chennai in Tamil Nadu and Hyderabad in Andhra Pradesh. The jihadi module of Al Qaeda had been supplying explosives and bomb making-material to many other states in India and several strategic locations in the adjoining Bangladesh. Soon after the National Investigation Agency took over investigation from West Bengal police, they found that the terror network (reportedly a jihadi module of Al Qaeda) had been supplying explosives and bomb making-material to many other states in India and several strategic locations in the adjoining Bangladesh. The probe revealed that the Simulia Madrasa of Burdwan had been actively recruiting and training hordes of jihadis from different parts of India as well as from the adjoining Bangladesh.

Investigations by the NIA confirmed that Islamic seminary called, Simulia Madrasa, had been functioning as a terrorist training camp. The police inquiries further revealed that the JMB was connected to a trans-Bengal jihadi network which had allegedly plotted blasts in Patna's Gandhi Maidan during the Prime Minister Narendra Modi's election meeting in the October, 2013. It was further confirmed that both Shakil Ahmed Ghazi (a Bangladeshi terrorist of JMB), who died in the blast at his home at Khagragarh (Burdwan district) while making bombs, and another suspect, Mohammad Qauser (who managed to escape to Bangladesh), were also involved in the blast at Chennai railway station on May 1, 2014. The timer used in the twin blasts in the Bangalore-Guwahati Express at Chennai Central Railway Station the timers used were similar to that which was found by the NIA in Burdwan. Mobile call records too indicated that several calls had been made by Shakil and Qauser to their contacts in Chennai in April, 2014. The sleuths of the central agency felt that JMB activists were in league with the Indian Mujahideen which had received outside help to carry out the blasts in Patna as well as Chennai.

Both in Patna and Chennai bomb blasts, the same timers had been used. In all probability, the terrorists also used the "Sigma" watches for timing the bomb blasts in both places. During searches at the home of Shakil and the injured terrorist Abdul Hakim at Khagragarh, a few 'Sigma' watches were reported to have been seized. After analysing mobile call records and cracking the fake e-mail IDs in a laptop found in the Khagragarh house, the sleuths discovered that Qauser had visited various states in South India. The SIM cards purchased in West Bengal were also used to make calls to their links in various states and even Bangladesh when the duo operated from Chennai just before the blasts.

Shakil's widow, Raziya Bibi admitted that her husband and Qauser had visited Chennai in April and May, 2014- just a few days before the blasts. The tags found in the time bombs in the train compartments tallied with the tags manufactured in West Bengal. The NIA team discovered that similar timers had been used in West Bengal bomb blasts. Prima facie this discovery confirms that the Patna and Chennai terrorists had connection with Shakil and Qauser. The seven bombs which exploded during the Patna rally in October, 2013, had been manufactured in West Bengal. In fact, one of the terrorists arrested from Barpeta in Assam, admitted having learnt to make IEDs in Jharkhand, where underground spynests of Indian Mujahideen and Al Qaeda had been strategically positioned by the militants, perhaps with the help of Pakistan's ISI.

Further investigations confirmed their links with some Indian Mujahideen operatives functioning from Karnataka. Raziya admitted that the two terrorists making calls to Abdul Qader Sultan Armar, who hailed from Bhatkal in Karnataka State. Now, however, Sultan Armar was operating from Waziristan in AFPAK region and adjoining Pakistan. Meanwhile, the NIA and other Central Intelligence Agencies continue their hunt for approximately 150 plus jihadis linked to Bangladesh module. The information received from various sources detailing the Simulia Madrasa terror apparatus revealed that the suspected ace-terrorist

Shakil Ahmed used to train self-motivated modules, who had gained expertise in making IEDs and carrying out terror strikes as independent operatives. Shakil was aided by two absconding suspects Sheikh Yusuf and Abdul. The Madarsa was reported to have trained more than 140 Muslim youth recruited from India as well as Bangladesh. Allegedly Shakil Ahmed was providing paramilitary training and giving lessons in the technology of making IEDs to new recruits in Simulia Seminary, which is an hour's drive from Burdwan.

The investigators seized several issues of The *INSPIRE* magazine, a well known publication of Al Qaeda, from the suspects' hideouts in Burdwan. The interrogation of captured Jihadi Hasan Molla revealed that *Inspire* magazine was an excellent guide for making lethal IEDs in kitchens. Al Qaeda magazines, especially *THE INSPIRE*, teaches how a bomb can be assembled from common items like cooking gas cylinders and iron nails. It can be set off by a remote controlled detonator.

According to reliable sources, substantial jihadi literature and printed material seized from the house of Shakil's relative Qader Sheikh's house had slogans like *"Jihad-from Bangladesh to Baghdad"* and similar radical promptings for indoctrination of trainees.

The repetitive incidents of numerous bomb blasts in West Bengal in 2014 and early 2015 shocked the security analysts and citizens alike. *Prima facie* while the West Bengal Police and intelligence agencies slumbered, Al Qaeda and its associate outfits like the Indian Mujahideen, Jamaat-ul—Mujahideen Bangladesh and the newly created IS Caliphate, acting in cohorts with the Inter Service Intelligence of Pakistan, succeeded in striking deep roots in various parts of West Bengal. Now it further stands confirmed that during the last ten years, the virus has spread to many other parts of the country. Thus, the eerie tale of the decades old illegal Bangladeshi infiltration continues to remain an unfinished narrative ! Period.

During the last three decades, the problem of continuous infiltration of Bangladeshis into Assam, West Bengal, Bihar, Orissa, and almost all north eastern states of India has assumed a weird shape. The alien infiltrators are now swarming all over the country and their massive presence is writ large across dozens of cities including Delhi, Mumbai, and even in far away Coimbatore and Chennai in Tamil Nadu. They have spread out to many small towns of states like Punjab, Haryana, Maharashtra, and Tamil Nadu.

Unfortunately, throughout the last three decades, India's political leadership has failed to realize that, just like Kashmir militancy, massive Bangladeshi infiltration has the potential to tear asunder the sociopolitical fabric of India. The north eastern region will be the first victim of this strategic 'tectonic tornado' unleashed by Pakistan's ISI, the reverbrations of which are now being felt all over the country.

Gigantic Dimensions of Illegal Infiltration

On a conservative estimate, the total number of Bangladeshi infiltrators and their progeny presently living in India could be anything between three to five crores, perhaps even more. Nine years ago, at a national convention on demography held at New Delhi in April, 2005, quite a few participants held the view that, by then, the total number of Bangladeshi infiltrators and their progeny could be as high as five crores. The mind-boggling dimensions of the problem were lucidly presented by Bibhuti Bhusan Nandy (a retired IPS officer of the Cabinet Secretariat) in a well-researched article titled, 'Space Invaders', published in *The Hindustan Times*, New Delhi on 14 February, 2003. In his brief research study, Nandy eloquently highlighted the fact that an analysis of Bangladesh's 1991 census data undertaken by Sarifa Begum (a demographer of the Bangladesh Institute of Development Studies, Dhaka) had revealed that there was an abnormally slow growth in the population of that country. The 1991 census disclosed that the total population of Bangladesh was 104.7 million, which indicated a clear shortfall of more than 10 million people. The actual headcount during 1991 census was at enormous variance with the estimate of 116–117 million for the decade projected by the United Nations Development Programme (UNDP) disclosing a huge shortfall of 13 million people. To everyone's amazement, the 1991 census headcount was found to be lower than even that of Bangladesh government's own moderate estimate of 112–13 million population for the 1991 census.

After an in-depth study, Sarifa Begum, a well-known economist and demographer, attributed the 'missing millions' to the unregistered 'outmigration' from Bangladesh. Through her meticulously researched analysis of the 1991 census data of Bangladesh, Sarifa Begum established that between 1981 and 1991 nearly 14 to 15 million Bangladeshis had outmigrated and entered India. That truth explained the massive shortage in the growth of population in Bangladesh

In another context, she had further estimated that nearly 3.5 million people had 'disappeared' from East Pakistan between 1951 and 1961, while another 1.5 million had possibly entered India between 1961 and 1974.[1] By inference, most of these five million migrants could be the persecuted Hindus, who were forcibly pushed out by jihadi outfits.

In any case, as per Sarifa Begum's estimate, the total number of outmigrated or missing Bangladeshis till 1991 could be around 19 million, to which must be added another two million Bangladeshi citizens, mostly residents of the districts bordering India, whose names were removed from that country's electoral rolls between 1995 and 1996. Obviously, those two million Bangladeshis could not have migrated to China, Australia, or Timbuktu. Common sense says that they just stealthily entered India through the unprotected, porous border. That adds to a grand total of 21 million people, who had managed to infiltrate into India by the year 1996. Unfortunately, since then, the influx has continued unabated. During the last 16 years, many more millions must have infiltrated into India. These figures, based on analytical studies conducted by Sarifa Begum, a Bangladeshi demographer, and Muslim by faith, highlight the dangerous magnitude of the security threat caused by illegal infiltration.

By now, the problem appears to have reached almost an irremediable stage, solely due to the complicity of India's sham-secular political tribe, who have persistently denied the roaring invasion of Bangladeshis, not only into Assam and West Bengal, but all across the country. A brief analysis of the data given below reveals the abnormally high percentage of growth in Muslim population in 13 border districts of Assam. It gives a clear idea of the massive deluge of alien infiltrators, which is playing havoc with the security of north eastern India and will surely overwhelm West Bengal, Bihar, Odisha, and Uttar Pradesh in perhaps as little as another two decades. The fast-paced demographic coup has already increased religion-based conflicts and growth of socio-economic tensions in the heartland states of Bihar and Uttar Pradesh.

Abnormally High Growth of Muslim Population in 13 Border Districts of Assam during the 1991-2001 Decade

District	*Percent-age in 2001*	*Percent-age in 1991*	*Decadal Growth*		*Ratio of Muslims to Hindus*
			Hindus	*Muslims*	
All Assam	30.92	28.43	13.9	29.3	2.10
1. Kokrajhar	20.40	19.33	5.2	19.1	3.65
2. Dhubri	74.30	70.48	5.9	29.6	5.01
3. Goalpara	53.70	50.19	12.8	31.7	2.48
4. Bongaigaon	38.50	32.74	2.3	31.8	13.57
5. Barpeta	59.40	56.06	9.7	25.9	2.67
6. Kamrup	24.80	23.38	23.5	33.7	1.43
7. Nalbari	22.10	19.94	9.2	25.2	2.75
8. Darrang	35.50	31.97	8.8	28.7	3.26
9. Marigaon	47.60	45.30	16.1	27.5	1.70
10. Nagaon	51.00	47.19	13.1	32.1	2.45
11. Cachar	36.10	34.50	15.4	24.5	1.60
12. Karimganj	52.30	49.17	13.6	29.6	2.16
13. Hailakandi	57.60	54.79	13.8	27.2	1.97
Average	46.87	43.32	12.97	28.56	2.20

Source: Compiled from data in Census 2001 and Census 1991 Reports.
Note : Religion-wise data of Census 2011 has been withheld by the Central Government without any explanation by the Registrar of Census.

In any case, the following conclusions are evident from the old data cited above :

- During the census decade 1991–2001, the percentage of Muslims in border districts of Assam had risen substantially by well over three percentage points, from 43.32 per cent in 1991 to 46.87 in 2001. It is significantly higher than the average Muslim presence of 30.9 per cent in Assam and their 13.4 per cent share in the population at the all-India level. Similarly, the ratio of Muslims to Hindus is much higher in border districts—

a natural corollary of the former's fast-paced growth, largely by the illegal influx, in addition to a higher rate of procreation among Muslim immigrants.

- It looks extraordinary that Bongaigaon District, located near the strategic 'chicken neck' area, recorded a phenomenal increase of nearly 5.8 per cent in Muslim population during the decade 1991–2001 due to illegal influx. A well-known United Liberation Front of Assam (ULFA) leader, Mithinga Daimary, who was caught during the joint operations by the Royal Bhutan Army and Indian security forces in December 2004, revealed that arms were being supplied to them from Bangladesh via a conduit running through Bongaigaon District. Daimary further confirmed that the weapons used to be smuggled from Bangladesh via the porous border of Meghalaya. Thus, there is a pressing need for assessing the likely geopolitical impact of the high growth of Bangladeshi Muslims in Bongaigaon District on the country's defence and internal security scenario because the 'chicken neck' is the lifeline sustaining our strategic link with the north eastern states. After the Kargil setback, Pakistan had enlisted the services of Muslim infiltrators swarming across Assam to tear away the entire north east from the rest of India by cutting off the 'chicken neck' connection between North Bengal and Assam.
- In the interest of national security, the reasons for the strategic Bongaigaon region near the 'chicken neck' developing into a Bangladeshi-Muslim dominated area need to be investigated and analysed in depth. Currently, no one can say for sure whether this dangerous demographic change is happening by sheer coincidence or by the Inter Services Intelligence's (ISI's)

well-planned demographic jihad against the *kaffir* India! At the same time, the causes of steep decline in the Hindu population of Bongaigaon District during the last decade need to be probed thoroughly and a determined effort made to halt it. *Prima facie* the hard-pressed Hindu community has been outmigrating from this area because of aggressive forays by Bangladeshi Muslims—at least that is what most Hindus of the area have been saying.

- During the decade 1991–2001, the growth rate of Hindus became abnormally low in six important districts of Bongaigaon, Kokrajhar, Dhubri, Barpeta, Nalbari, and Darrang, the lowest being in the Bongaigaon District where the Hindus grew barely 2.3 percent during 1991–2001 decade. In absolute numbers, the Muslims have grown 13.5 times faster than the Hindus in Bongaigaon District. This trend has far reaching implications because it clearly shows that the Hindus are migrating out in large numbers from the sensitive regions. There have been persistent reports that many Hindus have been sending away their womenfolk and children from several predominantly Bangla Muslim-dominated towns and villages of Assam and West Bengal. While departing from the Muslim-dominated areas, a sizeable number have been selling their land and property virtually at throwaway prices. The population statistics of these six districts of Assam, reflecting abysmally low Hindu growth rate, have confirmed what the late Bibhuti Bhusan Nandy had written more than 11 years ago, in an article in *The Hindustan Times*, New Delhi, in February 2003 and further reiterated in January 2005 in another article in *The Statesman*, New Delhi, about the plight of Hindus living in border districts.[1]

- The abnormally high decadal increase of 3.54 per cent in Muslim population in border districts translates into a Hindu/Muslim ratio of 1: 2.20, which shows that the Muslims have grown more than twice as fast as the Hindus. It vividly spells out the contours of the coming dangerous decades for the Indian nation in general and the Hindu identity of India in particular.

According to the 2001 census, an equally disquieting scenario is writ large across the following seven districts of West Bengal, as would be noticed from the data tabulated below.

Abnormal Rise in Muslim Population in Border Districts of West Bengal

Name of District	*Percent-age in 2001*	*Percent-age in 1991*	*Decadal Growth*		*Ratio of Muslims to Hindus*
			Hindus	*Muslims*	
All W. Bengal	25.3	23.6	15.1	25.9	1.71
1. Koch Bihar	24.2	23.3	12.8	18.6	1.45
2. Dinajpur (composite)	38.5	36.8	22.2	32.0	1.44
3. Malda	49.7	47.5	19.3	30.7	1.59
4. Murshidabad	63.7	61.4	16.1	28.4	1.76
5. Haora	24.4	22.2	11.2	26.0	2.32
6. Kolkata	20.3	17.7	0.7	18.9	29.09
7. S. Paragana	33.2	29.9	15.2	34.2	2.24
Average	37.5	34.5	12.5	28.7	2.29

Source: Compiled from the Census Reports of 1991 and 2001.
Note: Religion-wise data of Census 2011 has not been released so far.

Thus, the growth rate of Muslims in the border districts of West Bengal is also very high, though slightly lower than that of Assam. The two border districts of Murshidabad (Muslim population 63.7 per cent in 2001, that is, 13 years ago) and Malda (Muslim population 47.5 per cent in 2001, that is, 13 years ago) have reportedly become Muslim majority areas by now. The demographic change in the new district of North Dinajpur, where the Muslim percentage has risen to 47.4 per cent, appears to be equally worrisome. From the data tabulated above the following facts are established:

- As per the 2001 Census, the average decadal growth of 3.07 per cent in the Muslim population of border districts of West Bengal was much higher than the state average of 1.64 recorded during the previous decade, that is, in the 1991 Census. Evidently, the Muslims are growing at a much higher rate in border districts largely due to infiltration through a porous border, which is aided by the higher procreation rate of the Muslim community. It is a direct consequence of the massive infiltration from Bangladesh.
- Muslim growth is significantly higher in the southern districts of South Parganas and Kolkata, the decadal Muslim growth rate being 34.2 per cent in South Parganas, which was more than twice that of the Hindus at 15.2 per cent, and 18.9 per cent in Kolkata as against a measly 0.7 per cent of the Hindus. This phenomenon is partly explained by the abnormally low Hindu Total Fertility Rate (TFR) of one, which is far below the replacement level of 2.1. It raises the vital question of the likely over-acceptance of family planning by Hindus of West Bengal in general and by the *bhadralok*s of Kolkata in particular. Perhaps one reason for the pathetically poor Hindu growth in Kolkata could

be the sharp increase in popularity of condom-cum-abortion culture among the *bhadralok* urban Hindus on the pattern of communist Russia, and other demographically-dying countries of Europe, such as, Italy, Spain, France, and Germany. However, the Hindu TFR is quite low in rural areas of West Bengal, too.

- Yet another possible reason for the steep decline in Hindu growth rate could be that slowly and steadily the Hindus have started migrating out of Kolkata city, as was darkly hinted by Praful Goradia, in a thought-provoking article published in *The Pioneer*, New Delhi, in June 2005. Whatever may be the cause of the steep decline in percentage of the Hindu population, the ongoing demographic transformation will transform Kolkata into India's first Muslim majority metropolis within the next two to three decades! And most demographic and strategic experts agree with this foreboding prospect.

Nearly 13 years have elapsed since the 2001 census, and by now, many more districts of West Bengal, including Malda and Uttar Dinajpur, are believed to have become Muslim majority areas. Between 1951 and 2001, the Hindu population of West Bengal had declined by 5.7 percentage points, from 79.8 to 74.1 per cent, despite a huge influx of persistently persecuted Bangladeshi Hindus into West Bengal. During 1991–2001, the share of Muslims galloped ahead by a whopping 5.7 percentage points. As revealed by the 2001 census during the same decade, the Muslim growth rate in the state had quantum jumped to 28.7 per cent as compared to 12.5 per cent growth rate of Hindus. In other words, the percentage of Muslim growth in West Bengal during 1981–

1991 was more than twice the Hindu growth rate.

No wonder a seminally researched seminar paper by Dr Radhasyam Brahmachari, presented in *absentia* during a seminar held in January 2012 at India International Centre, was titled 'Dynasty of Hindus of West Bengal'. The seminar paper reads like a dirge for the dying Hindus of West Bengal. Incidentally, Dr Radhasyam Brahmchari is an euridite intellectual and a former Professor of Applied Physics in the Calcutta University.

According to press reports, a sealed affidavit filed in the High Court by Delhi Police stated that the capital alone was reported to have 13 million Bangladeshi infiltrators by September, 2003. Their numbers in Kolkata and Mumbai are massively higher.

The Government of Bangladesh is fully aware that millions of its citizens are outmigrating into India. It was highlighted by Baljit Rai in his book, *Demographic Aggression Against India,* that on 4 August 1991, the banner headline of *The Morning Sun*, a Dhaka based newspaper was 'One Crore People Missing'. The said headline was based on the mystery of the missing millions, as revealed by the analysis of 1991 the Census of Bangladesh. Could there be a more convincing and incontrovertible proof about the massive infiltration of Bangladeshis into India?

Additionally, Bibhuti Bhusan Nandy had provided irrefutable statistical evidence about the scale of illegal infiltration. Almost all Indian districts along the Indo-Bangaldesh border have recorded abnormally higher population growth. In sharp contrast, the corresponding adjoining districts of Bangladesh had witnessed equally abnormal lower population growth rates.

For instance, the Minister of State for Home Affairs, Sri Prakash Jaiswal, informed the Rajya Sabha on 14 July 2004, that the illegal infiltration from Bangladesh was of 'explosive proportions with illegal immigrants estimated at 1.2 crores.' While replying to a question by Datta Meghe, a Member of Parliament belonging to the Nationalist Congress Party of Sharad Pawar, he admitted that the number of infiltrators in Assam alone stood at 50 lakhs, while in neighbouring West Bengal, it was a staggering 57 lakhs. Astonishingly, within two weeks the same Minister made an abrupt about turn and declared in the house that the figures given in the earlier reply were 'hearsay'. But political observers were quick to point out that, soon after his 14 July, 2004, statement, the Minister had visited Assam where the State Chief Minister, Tarun Gogoi, had remonstrated with him for admitting the existence of infiltrators. That made the Minister renege on his previous statement within a few weeks by saying that the earlier figures were based on hearsay and that too from 'the interested parties'.

In a detailed report submitted in August 2000 by the Working Group on Border Management, headed by Madhav Godbole (a former Union Home Secretary having impeccable credentials), it was clearly stated that the number of illegal Bangladeshi immigrants was 1.5 crores at that time. It was further stated in the Working Group's detailed report that, on an average, at least three lakh illegal immigrants were entering India every year. The Working Group on Border was an officially constituted body and its report is packed with facts and figures collected from reliable official sources. Therefore, the figures of illegal Bangladeshis calculated by the Working Group could not have been dismissed as 'hearsay'. It is a mystery that when an authentic, well-documented, official report was readily available in the Home Ministry, from where did the then Minister of State for Home, Sri Prakash Jaiswal, obtain the 'hearsay' figure of 1.2 crore illegal Bangladeshis? Furthermore, when an official estimate confirming the presence of 1.5 crore illegal immigrants in the year 2000 was on the record of the Central Government, what made the Minister of State resort to lying in Parliament on the specious plea that the earlier figure of 1.2 crores was nothing more than hearsay? It is a pity that the two mutually contradictory replies of the Minister remained unchallenged in Parliament and that such patent falsehood was meekly accepted by our parliamentarians.

Long Years of Hostility and Strife in the Northeast

The three-decade-long bitter struggle by the indigenous Assamese against Muslim infiltrators has been increasing rapidly. The smouldering conflict between Bodos and the infiltrating Muslims has a long history of clashes arising out of the fierce attempts of infiltrators to snatch the land, jobs, livelihood, and productive resources of the Assamese people and several tribal communities of the northeast. The first high voltage conflict beteen the Infiltrators and the local tribals had occurred 30 years ago. Its origin goes back to February 1983, when a one-thousand-strong mob of Lalung tribals (called Tiwas) raided a huge cluster of Bangladeshi illegals at Nellie and killed more than 2000 Bangladeshi Muslim immigrants. Unfortunately, the Central Government refused to learn any lesson from that massive confrontation.

Ten years ago in 2004, a visiting Japanese researcher, Ms Makiko Kimura, had highlighted the growing tensions and clashes between the local people of Assam and the infiltrators by undertaking an an in-depth analysis of the following three narratives of the 1983 Nellie massacre:[3]

(i) Causes of the massacre, as narrated by the victims of the tragedy;

(ii) Causes of the Nellie clash, as explained by the attacking Tiwa (Lalung) tribals; and

(iii) Causes of the conflict leading to the massacre, as explained by the leaders of the Tiwa movement against Bangladeshi infiltrators.

After studying the genesis and gory aftermath of the Nellie massacre, the lady scholar from Japan drew attention to the high level of primordial suspicion and growing hostility between the indigenous people and the predators coming from a foreign land with a stamp of 'hostile culture'. The allusion to 'hostile culture' by Ms Kimura highlighted that it was a conflict between two colliding civilizations. She wrote that the Tiwa narratives powerfully reveal that the one major reason for the movements against aliens by the tribals of Assam was the seizure of their lands and economic resources by Bangladeshi invaders. She arrived at the conclusion that 'the movement is backed by the sense of deprivation among majority of the peasant tribes.'

Ms Kimura wanted to present her scholarly research at a seminar being organized at Guwahati towards the end of the year 2004 by the Omio Kumar Das Institute of Social Change and Development. But for reasons not altogether inscrutable, the permission for the proposed seminar was withdrawn by the Assam Government. Unfortunately, the resolve of the Assamese people, including tribal communities like Bodos, Karbis, and Lalungs, to resist the loss of land and economic resources was fully understood by Ms Kimura, but not by the selfish secular politicians of India. The situation is compounded by the communal and cultural differences between the Assamese and the intruders. Frankly, it is wrong to say that the Assam violence is not a communal clash. Ms Kimura's research clearly points to the primacy of both the communal and civilizational aspects of the ongoing conflict.

We are witnessing for the last three decades what is indeed a communal-cum-civilizational clash between the Assamese Hindus and Muslim infiltrators. Otherwise, during the 1912 clashes between Bodos and Bangladeshi Muslims, how dare Asaduddin Owaisi of Majlis-e Ittehad-ul-Muslimeen of Hyderabad issue a threat of retaliation by the Muslim community in the Indian Parliament? If it was indeed a non-communal issue, why would Badruddin Ajmal of All India Democratic Front (AIDUF) start a provocative war of words against the majority community? Why should the Chairman of the National Minorities Commission, Wajahat Habibullah, *post haste* dispatch a delegation headed by Syeda Hamid (not a member of the Minorities Commission) to Assam? If it was not a communal conflagration, why must Syeda Hamid, a member of the Planning Commission, make a provocative statement that it was an unequal fight between armed Bodos and inadequately-armed Bangladeshi Muslims and darkly hint that the latter might get weapons from jihadists to fight Bodos? Why would Muslim mobsters in Ranchi, Mumbai, Lucknow, and Allahabad go on a rampage and target the police and the Hindus? Why would the members of radical outfits like Popular Democratic Front and Raza Academy ignite communal tensions causing the flight of 50 thousand people belonging to the Northeast from Mumbai, Bangalore, Hyderabad, and Pune in 2012? Can the National Minority Commission explain why, in the ongoing conflict claiming more than 95 lives, the sympathies of most Indian Muslims are with illegal migrants? What is the rationale for Asauddin Owaisi and Syeda Hamid to rail against Bodos, among whom there are both Hindus and Christians?

The ugly re-run of clashes between infiltrators and local

Bodos, in which more than 100 lives were lost, took place in 2012. The first episode of conflict was caused by the books objecting to the construction of an illegal mosque on 29 May 2012, in Kokrajhar, by some radical Islamist outfits. Several Islamist outfits like All BTAD Minority Students Union (ABMSU) and United Muslim National Army, et cetera, tried to enforce a strike in the town, which caused the eruption of large-scale violence in which one Bangladeshi Muslim was killed in police firing. On 6 July 2012, some unidentified motorcyclists (suspected to be Bodos) shot dead two ABMSU activists in the Gossaigaon sub-division of Kokrajhar. Barely 11 days later, an attempt was made allegedly by Bodos to assassinate the former ABMSU President, Muheeb-ul Islam. Matters came to a head on 19 July 2012 when, in an organized assault by 1,000 Bangla Muslims, four Bodo youths were pulled out of a police van and lynched to death. The rumour that some young Bodos went missing while returning from an army recruitment camp and the news of the burning of a prominent Bodo shrine at Onthaibari near Gossaingaon led to an outbreak of large-scale rioting across Kokrajhar and the adjoining districts of Chirang, Baksa, and Bongaigaon in which the infiltrators became the prime targets of mob violence. Till now, more than 95 deaths have taken place and nearly five lakh persons uprooted from their homes and now huddled in hundreds of refugee camps. The total Bodo population is reported to be around 1.5 to two million. But unlike average Assamese, they are a hardy people, brave fighters, unwilling to let go of their lands and livelihood resources, and unwilling to yield to aggressive infiltrators.

According to Saitheshwar Brahma of Kasulata village of Kokrajhar, when he was young, there were only 10 Muslim families in their neighbourhood. He complained that now their number has grown to nearly one lakh Muslims spread around his village! Such indeed is the fear psychosis created by infiltrators that Samujjal Bhattachrya, an Advisor to All Assam Student Union (AASU), went to warn the Assamese people that soon Badruddin Ajmal of AIUDF might become the Chief Minister of Assam.

When millions of illegal migrants move from one country to another, they provoke massive anger, culminating in sociocultural tensions and clashes between the sons of the soil and the infiltrators. This is a historical process validated by innumerable narratives of civil wars across the globe caused by demographic changes (for example, in Lebanon, Kosovo. Bosnia, Serbia, et cetera). The wanton failure of the Indian government to understand this simple time-tested truth has led to the present civil strife in Assam and parts of the Northeast. No attempt was made by the Central Government to learn any lessson from the ghastly massacre at Nellie, which heralded regular clashes. During the last 20 years, nearly 15 militant Muslim outfits, aided by the ISI of Pakistan, have sprung up across Assam. The hostility of Bangladeshi immigrants to the Assamese life-style and their aggressive seizure of the land and livelihood of the local people has converted the State into a battlefield of two colliding civilizations.

While discussing the aggressive invasion of the Northeast by Bangladeshi infiltrators and its impact on communal harmony, it will be useful to understand the intensity of the feelings of the local population—I mean the anger of indigenous residents. A few years ago, during a frank, informal discussion amongest analysts and thinkers on the subject a retired paramilitary officer, belonging to the Northeast, bluntly asked us a question which foxed most participants. He asked point blank whether the Central

Government and the Indian political class would have dared to ignore the problem by looking the other way if millions of Pakistani Muslims had illegally entered North India through Punjab and Rajasthan? His question remained unanswered. I had no answer to his pesky but very rational question. Nor could anyone else among those present during the discussion dare answer it. The frankness of the questioner exposed the duplicity of the Central Government and highlighted the strong feelings of anger and alienation prevalent among the neglected people of Assam and other north eastern states. Frankly, the people of the north eastern region have developed a feeling of having been thrown to the wolves by the Central Government!

The worst fears about the long suspected intentions of Pakistan's ISI trying to infiltrate Bangladeshis for destabilizing the north eastern region came true when, in March 2003, three Bangladeshi infiltrators, were caught by the Dibrugarh police. The rowdy infiltrators confessed that they were taught to speak Assamese in Bangladesh before being smuggled into Assam. A more disturbing piece of information revealed during interrogation was that the prospective infiltrators were told beforehand that they would secure political patronage in Assam as long as they voted for a particular Indian political party. The three infiltrators were working as masons at a private campus in Jiban Phukan Nagar locality of Dibrugarh. One of them was a juvenile. He was the first to break down and confessed that he was from the Rongpur area of North Bangladesh and that he along with some others had been pushed into Assam three months ago. The two other infiltrators, both in their late 20s continued to tell the police that they were from Goalpara. But the cat was out of the bag when the juvenile infiltrator told the police that those two were also from

Bangladesh. Most infiltrators are taught a smattering knowledge of Assamese so that they can say convincingly that they are from Barpeta or Goalpara or some other town of lower Assam. They are largely engaged in manual labour, rickshaw pulling, or some similar profession. The police authorities invariably find it difficult to deport them as infiltrators often manage to get some kind of documents to prove their Indian identity.

The debate about the problem of illegal Bangladeshis has some very important constitutional and legal aspects centred around the ill-conceived and discriminatory legislation called Illegal Migrants (Detection by Tribunals) Act, 1983 (IMDT Act) which was declared *ultra vires* by the Supreme Court in July 2005. When elections to the Seventh Lok Sabha were held in Assam in January 1980, the State was in the grip of a mass agitation launched against illegal influx of Bangladeshis. A call had been given by the All Assam Students Union (AASU) and Assam Gana Parishad (AGP) to boycott the general election. Consequently, no elections could be held in 12 parliamentary constituencies out of a total of 14. In the entire state, elections had taken place for only for two constituencies, that is, Karimganj (reserved for Scheduled Castes (SCs) and Silchar, both located in Barak Valley, where there was practically no impact of the agitation against Bangladeshi infiltrators, because of their preponderance in the region. Subsequently, in 1983, the Election Commission decided to complete the electoral process in the remaining 12 constituencies, despite continuing unrest and tension in various parts of the state. Even then, elections could not be completed in seven out of the 12 constituencies due to the call for boycott. Despite all-out effort by the government, no election could be held in Brahamaputra Valley because of the highly disturbed law and order situation. In this manner, nearly half the constituencies of Assam remained unrepresented throughout the tenure of the Seventh Lok Sabha. Unfortunately, 'the black law', as the IMDT Act is popularly known in Assam, was passed by a Lok Sabha in which more than half of the Assamese electorate, concentrated in Brahamputra Valley, were not represented at all.

The most important constitutional enigma, however, was that, when a nationally applicable law known as the Foreigners Act was available in the statute book for detecting and deporting illegal immigrants, why did the government decide to pass another law for the same purpose and chose to restrict its promulgation to one state, that is, Assam alone?

The Illegal Migrant Detection by Tribunals Act, which came into force on 15 October 1983, was a patently infiltrator-friendly legislation. In flagrant violation of the universally accepted norm, the wonky law enacted by the Indian Parliament placed the onus of proving that the newly arrived foreigner was an illegal immigrant on the the complainant. To add insult to the injury, it stipulated that complainant should pay a token fee while lodging a complaint. The widespread agitation by the Assamese youth against the illegal influx was called off after the signing of the Assam Accord in August 1985 between the Central Government, the AASU and their allies, including the AGP, and the government of Assam. The tripartite agreement fixed 25 March 1971 (the day Bangladesh came into existence as an independent nation) as the mutually agreed date for detection and deportation of Bangladeshi infiltrators. It was accepted that those Bangladeshis, who entered Assam before that date would not be expelled and would become entitled for Indian citizenship in due course of time.

The Central Government also agreed to update the National Register of Citizens right upto the cut-off date. But that commitment made in the Assam Accord was never implemented because of manifest dishonesty on the part of the ruling politicians, who were hell-bent on capturing political power through vote-bank politics. Evidently, the law was conceived in political deception. It was nothing less than a fraud on the gullible people of Assam. Though crores of rupees were spent on setting up and sustaining a number of tribunals under the Act, the end result was pathetic. Not more than 1700 illegal immigrants were identified and deported by the government over two decades. No wonder widespread disaffection soon erupted among various sections of the indigenous population against the IMDT Act because of its inefficacy in deporting illegal immigrants. As resentment against the infiltration mounted and the intentions of the government became suspect, the All India Lawyers Forum for Civil Liberties filed a Public Interest Litigation (PIL) in the Supreme Court seeking deportation of illegal immigrants. It was followed by another PIL filed in the year 2000 by the AGP. Member of Parliament from Dibrugarh, Sarbananda Sonowal (former President of All Assam Students Union), praying that the IMDT Act be quashed because it was discriminatory against the Assamese and was totally unconstitutional. After prolonged legal battle in the Supreme Court Sonowal finally won; it was indeed a historic win. The Supreme Court gave its verdict on 12 July 2005, declaring the IMDT Act unconstitutional and *ultra vires*. In a stinging indictment of the government the Supreme Court made the following observations:

> A deep analysis of the IMDT Act and the Rules made thereunder would reveal that they have been purposely so enacted or made so as to give shelter or protection to illegal

> migrants who came to Assam from Bangladesh on or 25 March 1971, rather than to identify or deport them.

Drawing heavily upon the report sent by the then Governor of Assam, Lt. General Sinha, to the President on 8 November 1998, which stated that Assam was facing 'external aggression and internal disturbance' because of the silent invasion by illegal immigrants the apex court proclaimed in its judgement that the

> provisions of the IMDT Act and the Rules made thereunder clearly negate the constitutional mandate contained in Article 355 of the Constitution, where a duty has been upon the Union of India to protect every State against external aggression and internal disturbance. The IMDT Act which contravenes Article 355 of the Constitution is, therefore, wholly unconstitutional and must be struck down.

Among other things, the Supreme Court, in its 114-page long judgement, made the following *critical* observations:

- By enacting the impugned law, Parliament divested the Central Government of the legal authority to deport illegal Bangladeshi immigrants, whose growing numbers were creating a serious law and order problem in Assam.
- All over the world, the onus of proving that an individual was a bonafide national of the country of his or her domicile lies on the accused, while the IMDT Act shifted the burden of proof unfairly to the complainant and the state government.
- Illegal immigration was tantamount to 'external aggression' on the State of Assam, and therefore, in terms of Article 355 of the Constitution, the Central Government had a duty to protect Assam from external aggression and internal disturbances.

- The continuing immigration was responsible for impeding the economic growth of Assam despite immense natural resources possessed by the state.

The Supreme Court judgement raised politico-communal temperature in the State. The All Assam Minorities Students Union (AAMSU) gave a call for a state-wide strike on 13 July, 2005 which elicited good response in Muslim dominated districts of the state. It accused the Assam government of failure to defend the enactment of the IMDT Act and threatened to withdraw support to the ruling dispensation. Meanwhile, on 14 July, 2005, in a meeting chaired by the the former Prime Minister Dr. Manmohan Singh, the Central Government decided to set up a group of ministers to study the implications of the Supreme Court judgement, to hear the viewpoints of various groups and then recommend further action in the matter.

The verdict of the apex court was hailed by the Assamese people across the state, especially the students and youth groups. There were mass celebrations and Sarbananda Sonowal was given a tumultous welcome befitting a 'national hero' when he returned to Guwahati on 13 July, 2005. Rapturous crowds of thousands of youth lined up on both sides of the road when he came out of airport and proceeded to the city where a grand reception was held to felicitate him. Next day, when Sonowal visited Dibrugarh, the constituency he represented in the Lok Sabha, he was hailed as *Jatiya Bir*, a historic title associated with the legendary Ahom army general, Lachit Barphukan, famous for defeating the Muslim invaders in the battle of Saraighat in the year 1671 by sheer indomitable courage and military prowess.

The IMDT Act has been a source of legal battles for quite sometime. Most legal experts had questioned its constitutional or legal justification because of its discriminatory and anti-national nature. Yet, the Home Minister, Shivraj Patil, categorically refused to repeal it. When the former Prime Minister, Dr. Manmohan Singh visited Assam in November 2004, he too, refused to repeal the obnoxious law on the ground that it was needed for the protection of the minority community. The gratuitous plea advanced by the then Prime Minister Dr. Manmohan Singh and the then the Home Minister Shivraj Patil to retain the Act ran contrary to the reasons given for passing the legislation in the Statement of Objects and Reasons, which categorically stated that the Act was to be used only for detecting and deporting illegal immigrants and for protecting *the integrity and security* of the region.

How Anti-nationalist Politicians Sold Bharat to Alien Invaders

An alarming truth-giving clue to the most important secret of lakhs of Bangladeshis settling in Delhi, I mean the state secret of the political betrayal of the nation, has been provided by the late B.R. Lall, a former Director General of Police, Haryana, in his extensively researched book, *Free The CBI: Power Games in Bhopal & Other Cases*.

B.R. Lall was an upright scholarly police officer with impeccable credentials, who had served in the Central Bureau of Investigation with distinction. He died sometime ago due to sudden cardiac arrest. In Chapter 3 of his book, under the heading, 'Bangladeshis Settling in Delhi', Lall has given a brief, but copious, account of how, in 1988, nearly four lakh Bangladeshi infiltrators were permanently settled in Delhi and ration cards issued to them under the direct supervison of senior police officers and officials of the Delhi Administration, kowtowing to the diktats of the ruling policial dispensation.[4] B.R. Lall had come to Delhi in 1988 from Shillong to attend a conference on police-community relations hosted by the Delhi Police. A Sub-inspector of Delhi Police named Om Prakash was posted with him as a liaison officer. Lall was able to glean information from the Sub-inspector, on condition of confidentiality, that Bangladeshi infiltrators were being settled in Delhi by issuing ration cards on the spot, within hours of their reporting. In fact, Om Prakash, himself, was one of the officers unofficially deputed for facilitating their registration and settling down along the eastern bank of River Yamuna. He had been assigned the task of obtaining the fingerprints of the illegal infiltrators to ensure their identification in the event of their committing any crime in the future. B.R. Lall further learnt in confidence from Om Prakash that nearly four lakh such persons settled on the banks of River Yamuna had been issued ration cards by Delhi Administration and also unofficially recorded by the police as residents of Delhi. Being an irrepressible seeker of truth B.R. Lall raised this matter during the interaction in a session titled "Police at Crossroads". To his dismay, the issue was brushed aside by a senior officer on the dais on the ground that the matter had political overtones. When Lall persisted in seeking an answer to his question, his 'voice though not feeble' remained a cry in the wilderness.[4] He laments in his book that 'the great professionals on the dais consisting of luminaries of the police, the administration, media, academics all silently acquiesced to the accepted norm of golden silence.'[5] I am quoting below an excerpt from late B.R. Lall's book to apprise the readers of the anguish in his heart:

> Such is the mental slavery that if the people in power are not likely to relish or appreciate, the police will not take cognizance of such a fact, of whatsoever importance it may

> be to the society or the nation. Besides police, the administration was perhaps more obliging by issuing ration cards at an unheard of speed.[6]

The foregoing narrative reveals the methodology adopted by traitor politicians (appropriately called as 'Jaichandis' by a scholarly friend, who retired from Indian Foreign Service) to get the infiltrators registered as Indian citizens. The Hindi word *jaichandi* is the equivalent of the English word 'Quisling'. It may be recalled that Quisling was a widely despised traitor, who ruled over Norway during World War II and had stealthily conspired with Hitler to invade and seize his motherland.

Apparently, the sordid technique used by politicians ruling the country from Delhi was replicated by their counterpart vote-bank oriented traitors across India.

The truth about the political racket of settling millions of Bangladeshi infiltrators, recorded by a retired senior police officer in his book, gives a direct lie to the drummers of sham-secular falsehood, including the myopic left-liberal chatterati, shouting from their bandstands that there has been no infiltration by Bangladeshi Muslims.

The narrative of the late B.R. Lall also explains why in an affidavit filed in the year 2003 by Delhi Police in the Delhi High Court, the police had reportedly stated that the approximate number of Bangladeshi infiltrators residing in Delhi was around 13 lakhs !

It may be recalled that the late Bibhuti Bhusan Nandy, a senior officer who retired from the Research and Analysis Wing (RAW), kept on alerting the government for more than three years that, due to massive infiltration from across the border, more and more Hindu families were moving out from border areas virtually 'in droves'. They were moving out of border districts overrun by Bangla infiltrators, after selling their lands and houses at dirt cheap prices.

In this context, a very welcome development, though a grossly belated one, was the admission of the gravity of the situation by the former Chief Minister of West Bengal, Buddhadev Bhattacharjee. He was the only Marxist to publicly state that illegal immigrants were spreading 'the message of Islamic fundamentalism'. On 23 June 2005, while inaugurating a Border Security Force (BSF) seminar, he admitted that there was 'a serious problem with some of our neighbours'. He pointed out that 'Bangladesh says there are no Bangladeshis in India whereas the entire demography of certain parts of the country and West Bengal is being changed due to infiltration.' In many places, there were more Bangladeshi settlers than Indian, Buddhadev Bhattacharjee admitted. According to the former Chief Minister of West Bengal, three types of illegal immigrants were coming from Bangladesh. Firstly, there were groups, who spread the message of Islamic fundamentalism and campaigned for the rights of Muslims in Kashmir (located quite far away from Bangladesh). Secondly, there were groups that were directly involved in subversive activities. Thirdly, there as a group of north-Bengal based Kamtapur Liberation Organisation (KLO) militants, who had found shelter in Bangladesh after being driven out of Bhutan in December, 2003. The situation became so critical that the Governor of the state, Gopalkrishna Gandhi, described the relentless infiltration from Bangladesh as a 'time bomb'.

Buddhadev Bhttacharjee's concern was supported by Bimal Pramanik, Director, Centre for Research in Indo-Bangladesh Relations, Kolkata, who after analysing the 2001 Census data, came to the conclusion that unabated illegal infiltration through the porous eastern border was responsible for sharp changes in the demographic profile of

West Bengal. Equally important is the fact that many Bangladeshi immigrants have managed to acquire voting rights both in West Bengal and Bangladesh. The demographic disaster unfolding in Assam and West Bengal is nothing short of a massive fraud foisted on our innocent masses by political crooks, mostly secularized Hindus.

On a conservative estimate, it could be presumed that nearly 80 to 90 percent of Assam's Muslims happen to be illegal immigrants from Bangladesh. The 2001 Census revealed that the total population of Assam was 23,216,288 and 40 per cent of that figure comes to 9,286,512. Roughly, that could be the approximate number of Bangladeshis nestling all over Assam. On a rough count, by the 1990s, there were likely to be more than 90 lakh Bangladeshis in Assam alone. And that number is growing fast because the fertility rate of Bangladeshi Muslims is far higher than that of the Assamese Hindus, or for that matter, higher than the Hindus of West Bengal or Hindus of any other Indian state.

Due to a fast-changing demography, India's north-eastern region has already entered a phase of existential security crisis. It is amazing how our political leadership has been constantly denying the mind-boggling dimensions of Bangladeshi invasion and openly misleading the people by taking recourse to repetitive lying. There is no sense in blaming the Bangladesh government alone for denying the truth established so painstakingy by one of their own researchers about outmigration of 13 to 14 million Bangladeshis to India in one single decade of 1981–1991. Unfortunalely, our own political leaders are taking recourse to blatant lying about the gravity of the problem.

In another detailed report submitted years ago to the Central Government, Lt. General Ajai Singh, former Governor of Assam, had stated that, on an average, at least six thousand Bangladeshi infiltrators were entering the state every day, which adds up to nearly 22 lakhs infiltrators every year. It means that more than two crore infiltrators must have entered Assam alone within the last ten to twelve years.

True to his fundamentalist commitment to the politics of the minority vote-bank, the Chief Minister, Tarun Gogoi, promptly joined the issue with the Governor by denying that there was any large scale influx of illegal immigrants. Interestingly, if Sarifa Begum's figure of 14 million illegal immigrants entering India within one single decade of 1981–91 is juxtaposed with the figure given out by the former Assam Governor, it looks quite plausible that, by now, there could be nearly five crores illegal Bangladeshi immigrants living in India—a figure mentioned by more than one participant in a national convention on the 2001 Census held in Delhi in the last week of April, 2005. Yet, there is no dearth of Quislings *aka jaichandi*s decrying the Supreme Court's July 2005 judgement striking down the IMDT Act and terming the infiltration as invasion of India.

This dirty vote-bank politics of suicidal proportions is not confined to the political leadership of Assam or similarly threatened states like West Bengal and Bihar. It is practised and perfected by our purblind politicians right here in Delhi, the capital of our troubled nation, as exposed by the late B.R. Lall in his well researched tome.

Socio-economic Impact of Bangla Influx

During the last three decades, there has been a quantum jump in economic distress caused by growing unemployment all over the Northeast, especially in Assam. As mentioned by the Chief Minister of Assam in August 2004, there were more than two million unemployed youth in Assam alone, an abnormally high figure by national standards. It could be an underestimate because the State's economic survey for 2003–04 revealed that employment exchanges had 15,71,996 jobseekers. As a rule, the employment exchange figures are underestimated to the extent of 30 to 40 percent because the rural unemployed don't come to register themselves in Employment Exchanges. Obviously, the state has more than 20 to 25 lakh unemployed youth. Any guess what could be the jobs and livelihood resources usurped by Bangladeshis? Census 2001 had placed the population of Assam at 2,66,55,528. As per Census 1991, in Assam, the proportion of Assamese speaking populace was less than 40 percent indicating that they had already become a minority in their ancestral homestead. That should give us an idea of the size of Bangladeshi influx, which could be 70 to 80 lakhs. It means that at least 30 to 35 lakh jobs and livelihood resources which could have provided some relief to the local poor, have been usurped by Bangladeshis in Assam alone.

Across India, among the poorest sections of society, at least two members of the family (often both father and mother) work to keep the kitchen fires burning. Thus, Nandy is not far wrong in saying that by pushing 15 per cent of its population into India, Bangladesh has imposed a heavy financial and economic burden on Indian citizens. And this burden is borne by the poorest of the poor living on the margin of starvation because they are the first victims of the loss of small-time jobs and livelihood sources, eagerly chased by infiltrators. The mutiple cases of clashes between the Bodos and the Bangla immigrants show that Assam is getting ready for a major conflagration between the two colliding civilizations.

The diehard 'doubting Thomases' and armchair

philosophers of New Delhi, unwilling to accept the truth, will do well to undertake a tour of the border districts of Assam and Bangladesh and interact with the original residents of the border villages, now outmigrating due to fear. The visiting politicians to the Northeast will come back to Delhi infinitely wiser and sober.

There is an urgent need to publicly debate the anti-national role of several purblind politicians and outfits acting unintelligently to indirectly facilitate undermining the security and sovereignty of the Indian nation by the ISI of Pakistan. Pakistan's role in promoting jihad against India, through trained terrorists, can be ignored only at great peril to the security of the Indian nation and life and property of citizens. The possibility of stepping up the ongoing jihad against India through the Indo-Pakistan frontier in Northwest has been substantially reduced during the last ten years due to the following reasons:

(i) Extensive fencing along the Indo-Pakistan border and the line of control has significantly reduced the scope for large-scale infiltration and attempts at waging proxy war against India, excepting the State of Jammu & Kashmir (J&K).

(ii) After 9/11, the extensive presence of US intelligence sleuths in Pakistan has made it difficult for the ISI to openly carry out anti-India campaigns through the Punjab and/or Rajasthan border.

(iii) After the Kargil war, India has increased the level of vigil on the Indo-Pakistan Border, especially in J&K State, thus making the task of large-scale infiltration into India difficult.

(iv) In the circumstances, Pakistan has fine tuned its old strategy of waging the 'war of a thousand cuts' against India by shifting ISI's focus to infiltration

> of jihadi warriors and spies through the porous Indo-Bangladesh border. No wonder, in recent years Bangladesh has become the major operational ground for waging a proxy war against India. Pakistan's ISI and Al Qaeda have a grand design to set up a caliphate from Indonesia to the Balkans through Malayasia, Thailand, Bangladesh, via India and through Pakistan right into the Balkans. In this global Islamic design, India is the only bulwark, populated by non-Muslims, against the Islamic dream of a trans-Asian caliphate. In this gigantic endeavour, a number of Jihadi organizations like Harkat-ul-Jihad-e Islami Bangladesh (HUJI-B), Jamat-e-Islami, and Okiya Jote, duly aided by Assam-based militant outfits like the Muslim Liberation Tigers of Assam, Islamic Liberation Army of Assam, Muslim Security Force, Al Jihad-e Islami, and Adam Sena, have joined hands to make an attempt at tearing away Assam and some other parts of the Northeast from the Indian Republic. In fact, HUJI-B was clearly involved in the 2002 terror attack on the American Center in Kolkata. In recent years Jihadi operators belonging to HUJI-B are believed to have been involved in the 2006 attack on Sankat Mochan temple, Varanasi, the Mumbai bomb blasts, the twin blasts in Hyderabad last year and the latest bomb blasts in Jaipur, Rajasthan. Consequently, in the first week of March 2008, the US government declared HUJI-B as a Foreign Terrorist Organisation FTO).

An important instance of the perfidy of Bangladesh-based Jihadis attacking the the Hindu ethos was the dastardly attack on the makeshift Ramjanambhoomi temple on 15 July 2005, which was planned in Bangladesh. One of the masterminds was Maqbool Hussain, a Dhubri born Jaish-e-Mohammad Jihadi terrorist and a close confidante of the notorious Maulana Azhar Masood, chief of Jaish-e-Muhamad. Maqbool was arrested on 29 October, 2005 by Delhi Police along with his associate Adnan, a Pakistani national and seasoned Jihadi warrior. Originally from Assam, Maqbool had taken up residence in Dhaka and used to operate under different identities. The code name assigned to him by JeM was Zahid, while in Bangladesh he was known as Anwar. After travelling to Karachi on forged documents, Maqbool had even met Masood Azhar at Bahawalpur. He had studied for five years at the great fount of Jihadi terrorism, Deoband in India, from 1992 to 1997. Similarly, one of the masterminds of the Sankat Mochan bomb blast at Varanasi in March 2006, the Pesh Imam of a mosque in Allahabad (UP), too, had studied at Dar ul-Uloom, Deoband, and had allegedly a Bangladesh connection.

Out-of-the Box Suggestions for Tackling the Menace of Infiltration

To be candid, till date, neither the Central Government, nor the state government has ever tried to tackle the problem in a serious manner. Even at this late stage, the problem is not totally intractable, provided we do some out-of-box thinking. The following steps can substantially alter the scenario and help in protecting our shrinking border.

1. Apart from making a concerted attempt across the country to identify and deport all Bangladeshi infiltrators, a crash programme of resettling ex-servicemen and retired paramilitary personnel all

along the Indo-Bangladesh border should be undertaken. A well-planned string of 'Sentinel Settlements' of ex-servicemen should be set up along the Indo-Bangladesh border. As far as possible, the settlers should be from the north-eastern region itself, but they must be financially supported by the government to buy farmland and licensed arms for defending their farms/orchards and the adjoining border areas. For better management and prompt results, cooperatives of 'sentinel settlements' should be patterned on the Israeli concept of the 'armed kibbutz'. The settlers must be fully armed and well-equipped to take on the Jihadi infiltrators. In due course of time, such 'sentinel settlements' should be set up along all our borders, including the Indo-Pak border in Gujarat, Rajasthan, and Punjab—even all along the Himachal Pradesh border adjacent to the Doda-Kishtwar region of J&K.

2. The entire border with Bangladesh should be protected with a high-tech fortified Security Barrier (not ordinary concertina fencing), dotted with multiple electronic sensors and machine-gun-mounted watch towers as add-ons. For the proposed security barrier, expert advice of Israeli engineers should be sought. They have constructed a virtually impregnable barrier-cum-fence to prevent Palestinian suicide bombers from entering Israel.
3. It is time that the Government of India enacted and enforced a stringent law prohibiting employment of any 'illegal foreigner', as has been done by the Government of United Kingdom. Like the United

Kingdom, the Indian law should impose on-the-spot fine of one lakh rupees on those, who give employment to any foreigner entering India. Under the British law titled the Immigration, Asylum and Nationality Act, passed in 2006, an employer giving a job to any illegal immigrant is liable to be fined 2000 pounds stirling (equivalent of Indian Rs. 1,60,000) on the spot every time an illegal immigrant is employed. Also, finger printing of all suspected illegal immigrants should be made compulsory. If the governments of UK and several other countries can enact such laws, why cannot India do that? In the Indian law, a provision should also be incorporated for punishing all illegal immigrants taking up a job or occupation in India, without obtaining the prior permission from the Central Government. That would make it more stringent and deter all attempts at infiltration.

4. The long pending task of registration of all Indian nationals should be completed at an early date. It should be done first and foremost in Assam, West Bengal, and all the north eastern states. Every Indian citizen should be issued a photo-ID card and there should be full documentation of all foreigners, legal as well as illegal. This high priority task should be implemented expeditiously, without delay.
5. Another important measure to counter the menace will be to motivate people to boycott Bangladeshi hawkers, vendors, and rickshaw-pullers, as was done in May 2005, by a vigilant youth group of Dibrugarh, known as Chiring Chapori Yuva

Manch, which made thousands of infiltrators flee from that district. In fact, public opinion needs to be mobilized across the country to boycott all Bangladeshi infiltrators by denying them jobs, residential accommodation, and refusing to have any dealings with them.

NOTES

1. Nandy, Bibhuti Bhusan, 'Secular Claims', *The Statesman*, New Delhi, 25 January 2005.
2. Sinha, Bhadra, 'Can't Deport Bangladeshi Immigrants', *The Times of India*, New Delhi, 25 September 2003.
3. 'Assam Bans Nellie Case Presentation', *The Asian Age,* New Delhi, 14 November 2004.
4. Lall, B.R., *Free The CBI: Power Games in Bhopal & Other Cases*, p. 79.
5. Ibid.
6. Ibid, p. 81.

REFERENCES

1. Lall, B.R., *Free The CBI: Power Games in Bhopal & Other Cases*, pp. 79-81.
2. Ibid.
3. Ibid.
4. Sinha, Bhadra, 'Can't Deport Bangladeshi Immigrants', *The Times of India*, New Delhi, 25 September 2003.

Notes on Contributors

Bhaskar Roy is a former Joint Secretary of the Cabinet Secretariat, Government of India. Subsequently, he served as the Centre Director, NTRO. Having worked in the media and the publishing industry, he joined the government and served abroad. His interests include Bangladesh, China and other areas of strategic interest. Currently, he is a consultant on strategic issues with South Asia Analysis Group (SAAG).

Kalyan K. Mitra IPS (Retd) served in the R&AW. He was the Director, Aviation Research Centre and retired as the Principal Director, D.G. Security, Cabinet Secretariat. He has published numerous articles on strategic issues and written a monograph *India, China and South East Asia*. He is convener, Security Studies in 'Surya Foundation', a New Delhi-based Think Tank and Member Editorial Board of *Defence Watch*, a monthly journal. He has been awarded "Police Medal" for Meritorious Service as well as "President's Police Medal for Distinguished Service". Shri Mitra has won "Sangram Medal" and "Poorvi Star" for services rendered during the Indo-Pak War in 1971.

A.K. Verma, a former Secretary to the Government of India, headed the Research and Analysis Wing of the Government of India for almost three years from July, 1987 to June, 1990. He has also experience of other branches of the Government, having been associated at different periods of his career with the Ministry of External Affairs and Ministry of Information and Broadcasting. He frequently participates in various discussions on TV channels. Currently, he is a Member, Advisory Board, Vivekanand International Foundation, New Delhi. He is also a former President of Association of Retired Senior Indian Police Service Officers (ARSIPSO).

B.S. Das belongs to the first batch of IPS officers with a record of multifarious involvement in domestic and international security with a diplomatic contribution. He is a fairly well-known author on current affairs specially, covering events in Sikkim and Bhutan.

Prakash Singh is a renowned police officer of UP cadre. He was the Director General of Police of UP and Assam and the Director General of the Border Security Force. He has authored many books. His professional articles on and security police problems and issues appeared in different newspapers and journals.

S.K. Datta, a distinguished police officer, who served long years in CBI and held the post of the Director.

Sankar Sen is a distinguished member of the Indian Police Service. He was the Director of National Police Academy, Hyderabad and Director General of the National Human Rights Commission. He was awarded Police Medal for Meritorious Services and President Medal for Distinguished Service. He has authored a number of books and his articles appear in well known newspapers, magazines and journals in and outside the country. Presently he is a Senior Fellow at the Institute of Social Sciences, New Delhi.

Shyamal Datta, an IPS officer of 1965 batch, belonging to West Bengal cadre, joined the Intelligence Bureau (IB), Government of India, New Delhi in 1979. After serving as the

Director, Special Protection Group (SPG), looking after security of the Prime Ministers, he was elevated to the post of Director, IB in 1998 wherefrom he retired in 2001. Later, he became Governor of Nagaland in January, 2002 and demitted office in February, 2007. He now writes pieces, lectures on subjects of internal security, political developments and intelligence.

Vikram Sood, a career intelligence officer, retired in March, 2003 after heading India's external intelligence service, the Research and Analysis Wing. He is currently Adviser, Observer Research Foundation. He has been writing regularly on security, foreign relations and strategic issues in various Indian newspapers and foreign journals. He has contributed chapters on security, intelligence, terrorism and geopolitical issues to books/journals.

B.L. Vohra is an officer of the 1967 batch of the Indian Police Service. He had earlier served with distinction in Delhi, Punjab, J&K and Manipur in different capacities in para-military forces. He has been the Director General of Civil Defence and Seema Suraksha Bal. He is the recipient of the President's Police Medal for Distinguished Service, besides other medals and honours. He has authored many books and now trains executives in soft skills.

D.C. Nath (1960-WB) superannuated from the Intelligence Bureau as the Special Director in 1995. He was then in the corporate world of Industrial Security for over 14 years between 1996 and 2011. The article is based on, his personal experience.

D.C. Pathak, a distinguished member of the Indian Police Service (1960- Rajasthan), spent most of his career in Intelligence Bureau. After serving in various capacities, he became Director Intelligence Bureau—a position he held with great distinction. After retirement he was appointed a member of the National Security Advisory Board. Shri Pathak is a strategic analyst of repute who writes regularly for newspapers and journals. He has written three books on Intelligence which have been well received.

Ram Kumar Ohri is a retired IPS officer and a former Inspector General of Police, Arunachal Pradesh. In recognition of his varied experience and professional competence, he was decorated with the Police Medal for Meritorious Services and the President's Medal for Distinguished Service. His articles and research papers are published in different newspapers and journals. Presently, Ram Ohri is associated with "Patriots' Forum" a Delhi-based Think tank.